Dr. Kholoud Al-Qubbaj

Acculturation Among Arabic Children And Their Families In The U.S.A

Dr. Kholoud Al-Qubbaj

# Acculturation Among Arabic Children And Their Families In The U.S.A

Acculturation Among Arabic Children And Their Families In The United States: Some Educational Considerations

LAP LAMBERT Academic Publishing

**Impressum/Imprint (nur für Deutschland/ only for Germany)**
Bibliografische Information der Deutschen Nationalbibliothek: Die Deutsche Nationalbibliothek verzeichnet diese Publikation in der Deutschen Nationalbibliografie; detaillierte bibliografische Daten sind im Internet über http://dnb.d-nb.de abrufbar.

Alle in diesem Buch genannten Marken und Produktnamen unterliegen warenzeichen-, marken- oder patentrechtlichem Schutz bzw. sind Warenzeichen oder eingetragene Warenzeichen der jeweiligen Inhaber. Die Wiedergabe von Marken, Produktnamen, Gebrauchsnamen, Handelsnamen, Warenbezeichnungen u.s.w. in diesem Werk berechtigt auch ohne besondere Kennzeichnung nicht zu der Annahme, dass solche Namen im Sinne der Warenzeichen- und Markenschutzgesetzgebung als frei zu betrachten wären und daher von jedermann benutzt werden dürften.

Coverbild: www.ingimage.com

Verlag: LAP LAMBERT Academic Publishing AG & Co. KG
Dudweiler Landstr. 99, 66123 Saarbrücken, Deutschland
Telefon +49 681 3720-310, Telefax +49 681 3720-3109
Email: info@lap-publishing.com

Herstellung in Deutschland:
Schaltungsdienst Lange o.H.G., Berlin
Books on Demand GmbH, Norderstedt
Reha GmbH, Saarbrücken
Amazon Distribution GmbH, Leipzig
**ISBN: 978-3-8383-7498-7**

**Imprint (only for USA, GB)**
Bibliographic information published by the Deutsche Nationalbibliothek: The Deutsche Nationalbibliothek lists this publication in the Deutsche Nationalbibliografie; detailed bibliographic data are available in the Internet at http://dnb.d-nb.de.

Any brand names and product names mentioned in this book are subject to trademark, brand or patent protection and are trademarks or registered trademarks of their respective holders. The use of brand names, product names, common names, trade names, product descriptions etc. even without a particular marking in this works is in no way to be construed to mean that such names may be regarded as unrestricted in respect of trademark and brand protection legislation and could thus be used by anyone.

Cover image: www.ingimage.com

Publisher: LAP LAMBERT Academic Publishing AG & Co. KG
Dudweiler Landstr. 99, 66123 Saarbrücken, Germany
Phone +49 681 3720-310, Fax +49 681 3720-3109
Email: info@lap-publishing.com

Printed in the U.S.A.
Printed in the U.K. by (see last page)
**ISBN: 978-3-8383-7498-7**

Copyright © 2010 by the author and LAP LAMBERT Academic Publishing AG & Co. KG
and licensors
All rights reserved. Saarbrücken 2010

## TABLE OF CONTENTS

|  | Page |
|---|---|
| LIST OF TABLES | xiv |

Chapter

| 1. INTRODUCTION | 1 |
|---|---|
| Background of the Study | 1 |
| Purpose of the Study | 2 |
| Significance of the Study | 2 |
| Research Questions | 4 |
| Definition of Terms | 5 |
| Population and Culture | 7 |
| Background of the Arab World | 13 |
| Arabic Language | 15 |
| Chapter Summary | 18 |
| 2. LITERATURE REVIEW | 19 |
| Acculturation | 19 |
| Acculturation Models | 27 |
| Stereotyping | 31 |
| Theoretical Frameworks | 34 |
| Chapter Summary | 41 |
| 3. METHODOLOGY | 42 |
| Naturalistic Paradigm of Research | 42 |

Chapter         Page

| | |
|---|---|
| Evaluation versus Research | 43 |
| Definition of Evaluation | 46 |
| Evaluation Standards | 46 |
| Evaluation Models: CIPP as a Research Tool | 47 |
| Qualitative Procedures: CIPP Model of Evaluation as a Tool of Research | 49 |
| The Setting | 57 |
| Population | 60 |
| Participant Observation: Naturalistic Observation | 62 |
| Documentation | 64 |
| Interviewing | 65 |
| Focus Group | 66 |
| Data Analysis (from the CIPP model) | 68 |
| Triangulation of Summative Research | 69 |
| Confidentiality and Protection of Subjects Privacy | 69 |
| Summary | 70 |
| 4. FINDINGS | 71 |
| Curriculum and Assimilation: CIPP Research of Language and Culture | 74 |
| Interviews with Students of Middle and High Schools: CIPP Research | 79 |
| Interviews with Teachers: CIPP Research | 84 |

| Chapter | Page |
|---|---|
| Focus Group Interviews: CIPP Research | 89 |
| Language Preference: CIPP Research | 92 |

|   |   |
|---|---|
| Cultural Preference: CIPP Research | 95 |
| Cultural Preference of Parents | 97 |
| Cultural Preference of Adult Children | 98 |
| Summary | 99 |
| 5. IMPLICATIONS AND RECOMMENDATIONS | 100 |
| Implications | 100 |
| Recommendations | 106 |
| Limitations of the Study | 112 |

Appendices

| | | |
|---|---|---|
| A. | ARAB WORLD MAP | 115 |
| B. | INTERVIEWING USING SEIDMAN PROCEDURE WITH 4 TUTORS, 14 TEACHERS, 3 PRINCIPALS | 116 |
| C. | OPEN-ENDED INTERVIEW QUESTIONS WITH STUDENTS OF MIDDLE AND HIGH SCHOOLS | 117 |
| D. | FOCUS GROUP QUESTIONS FOR (FATHERS GROUP) OF 15 PARENTS OF PRE-SCHOOL, ELEMENTARY, MIDDLE AND HIGH SCHOOLS STUDENTS | 118 |
| E. | OPEN-ENDED INTERVIEW QUESTIONS OF LANGUAGE PREFERENCE WITH STUDENTS AND THEIR PARENTS | 119 |
| F. | OPEN-ENDED INTERVIEW QUESTIONS OF CULTURAL PREFERENCE WITH STUDENTS AND THEIR PARENTS | 120 |

| | |
|---|---|
| REFERENCES | 122 |

## LIST OF TABLES

| Table | Page |
|---|---|
| 1. CIPP Model | 56 |
| 2. Focus Group | 57 |
| 3. Settings | 59 |
| 4. Family Groups | 62 |
| 5. Findings (Summative Research) | 77 |
| 6. Study Sample of Middle and High School Students | 83 |
| 7. Teachers Group | 88 |

# HAPTER 1

# INTRODUCTION

**Background of the Study**

The process of acculturation has been defined and redefined many times over the past sixty years. Redfield et al. in Ponterotto (2001) defined acculturation as:

> Acculturation comprehends those phenomena which results when groups of individuals sharing different cultures come into continuous first-hand contact, with subsequent changes in the original culture patterns of either or both groups. (pp. 394-421)

Acculturation is the concept that allows us to understand the similarities and differences among the ethnically diverse populations. We are all ethnically diverse coming from different backgrounds, which have been integrated into the people we are today. Due to historical, cultural, educational, and political reasons, minority populations have not been allowed to integrate at the same level as the majority culture into mainstream society (Ponterotto, 2001).

Acculturation is a major concern facing Arabic students in the public schools of the United States. The effects and influences that the acculturation process has on Arabic students and their families within the educational system cannot be ignored. As a member of the Arabic community in the New Mexican Pecan Valley area and as a parent of children in the public school system, my interest in how acculturation and assimilation affect Arabic students was piqued. Indeed, the number of Arabic students in the Pecan Valley area has increased significantly since my arrival in 1993, but despite this occurrence, no measured action regarding the Arabic culture and language has been considered. Consequently, I have found it necessary to initiate a study in order to better understand the effects that acculturation has on the learning processes of these students; in turn, I have discovered the impact that it can have on both the students and their families, especially when they return to their native countries and attempt to help their people. My interest in this research project also developed from studying multicultural, critical, and Freirean theoretical approaches that provide classification regarding cultural domination. These theories offer a change from traditional methods of teaching to student-centered learning environments that utilize problem-posing methods for developing critical thinking habits.

**Purpose of the Study**

The purpose of this study was to research the acculturation of Arabic students, a process that historically school systems have adopted in order to homogenize the identities of minorities to those of the dominant culture (Feagin & Booher, 2003). This study outlines the needs of Arabic students in North American society, noting the positive and negative consequences that national standardized curriculums have on sample populations of Arabic students and their parents in Pecan Valley, New Mexico; Green City, New York; Hot City, Texas; and Intermountain City, Utah.

**Significance of the Study**

This was the first attempt to study the acculturation processes of Arabic students in the Pecan Valley, New Mexico educational system, an important undertaking when considering Nassar-McMillan and Hakim-Larson's (2003) statement that there have been no extensive or systematic studies on the Arab American communities within the United States. My study considers how the Arab American's linguistic and cultural needs are being addressed in public education, focusing on the parents' wishes that their children maintain their cultural heritages.

As a member of the Arab American community within the United states, a mother of public school educated children, and a teacher, I feel that a study on the acculturation processes of Arabic students in the public school system is extremely important and timely. By providing information on the positive and negative effects that acculturation can have on the Pecan Valley Arabic students, I provide information that will determine the future of program planning nationwide in the school curriculums, consequently addressing the needs of Arabic students and recommending ways that they can maintain their cultural heritages while attending the public schools in the United States.

In order to accomplish these aims, I examined how the media and school textbooks categorize Arab Americans, creating stereotypes that embed themselves into the American consciousness. S. Jarrar (1983) explains that the depictions of Arab Americans in the media have caused them to "suffer from malevolent and inaccurate characterization" (p. xv). He also describes a study that examined 58 elementary and junior high textbooks, noting that they were filled with misconceptions about the Arab culture; the textbooks did so through

1. Inaccurate statements.
2. Misleading statements.

3. Incomplete statements which led, at times, to a wrong impression.
4. Omissions of important facts about the Arabs and about famous characters in Arab culture.
5. Information that in many cases was not brought up-to-date in new editions of textbooks. (pp. 382-83)

Al-Khatab (1999) explains "misinformation and lack of information about their [Arab American] culture and heritage play a significant role in the formation of American perception and understanding of Arab American students." Thus, when placed in the mainstream of classrooms, Arab American children "are confronted by preconceived prejudices and biases about the Arab people."

**Research Questions**

For this qualitative study on the acculturation of Arabic students and their families in the United States, based upon my assumptions of the process of acculturation of Arab Americans, the following questions were used to research the Arabic students, their parents, and the teachers in the public school systems.

1. How much acculturation from a culture and a language point of view do Arabic students face in the public schools and nationwide?
2. What are some of the challenges Arabic students encounter in their schooling processes in the United States?
3. Do these difficulties change the parents', students', and teachers' learning environments?
4. Does ignoring the Arabic language and culture influence the parents and their children in the public schools?

In answering these question The CIPP Model of evaluation was used as a tool to investigate the acculturation process of Arab American families and their children in culture and language in the United States. The CIPP model is modified from the original model initiated in the 1960s by Daniel Stufflebeam in order to meet my research qualitative measurements to study the samples of families, children, teachers and focus group. Since the 1960s, the researchers modified this model to meet their research investigations.

**Definition of Terms**

I have defined the following terms based on my knowledge of the Arabic culture. As a member of the Arabic community, my understanding of this culture is expansive, and the following words or terms are important elements for understanding this culture. Also, I have structured the content of my definitions for Arabs, the Arabic family, cultural shock, ethnocide, Islam, and the Islamic Center by referring to Patai's (2002) understanding of these terms:

Arabs are natives of Arabic Middle Eastern countries; Palestine, Jordan, Lebanon, and Syria comprise the Arab speaking states of the Eastern Mediterranean Sea. The Arabian Gulf countries are comprised of Saudi Arabia, Oman, Qatar, Kuwait, Iraq, Yemen, Bahrain, and the United Arab Emirates. Egypt, Sudan, Somalia, and the Northwestern portion of Africa--Morocco, Mauritania, Libya, Algeria, and Tunisia--make up the rest of the Arab World.

The Arabic Family is a unit that consists of parents and their children. The unit shares the same Arabic language and culture. Also, the unit has the same common origin of Middle Eastern countries. In Arabic families men and women are equal, but with different rules originated from Islamic rules. A more conservative minimum dress code for both men and women is required. A man must always cover his body between the navel and the knee. A woman must cover everything but her face and hands and obscure the details of her body from public. Men are responsible for maintaining, protecting, and supporting the family, while women are not primarily responsible even if they are married.

Cultural Shock is the sudden effect on the mind and emotions caused by cultural differences.

Ethnocide is the eradication of an ethnic group because one culture feels superior over another ethnic group's culture.

Islam is the willful and complete submission to the one and only creator, Allah, and to live in peace with him, one's self, society, and environment. Islam comes from the Arabic word meaning submit and surrender. It is the Muslim faith, as set forth by the Quran, a record of the exact words of Allah, a message sent to the Prophet Muhammad by the Angel Gabriel.

The Islamic Center is the Muslims place of worship. It is also called a Mosque or a masjed.

**Population and Culture**

The major populations targeted for this acculturation study were Arabic students attending the Pecan Valley, New Mexico public schools, the Islamic Center of Pecan Valley, and the respective families of these students. In addition, Arabic students and families from Green City, New York, Intermountain City, Utah, and Hot City, Texas were included in the research. The study's students attended schooling levels ranging from pre-school to high school, and the populations included both male and female subjects from twenty-five different families. In some cases, at least one, sometimes both, of the students' parents attended New Mexico State University (NMSU), and a majority of these students had lived in NMSU student family housing. Also, both parents of these families had either managed their own business or worked in a teaching profession at the university or college levels; some were also doctors employed by the local hospitals, and most of the families had pre-school, elementary, middle, or high school level children.

Generally, all of the students' families originated from Arabic countries; however, the study also included Arabic American students with Arabic nationalities because they too shared similar linguistic and cultural heritages. The various families were citizens, non-citizens, or resident aliens of the United States, coming from different areas of the Middle East, some of which were Palestine, Jordan, Egypt, Algeria, Sudan, Saudi Arabia, United Arab Emirates, Yemen, Oman, Qatar, Syria, Libya, and Iraq.

For the most part, the study's parents preferred multi-cultural ideologies over linguistic and cultural assimilation, mainly because it allowed their children to maintain their Arabic heritages, both culturally and linguistically. Lambert and Taylor (1990), after observing Hamtrack, Michigan Arab, Albanian, and Polish groups, note this preference, stating:

> Arab parents endorse more strongly than others the use of their heritage language in the community and public schools. Moreover, Arab parents feel that all ethnic groups should be able to use the native language beyond the family confines. Thus, we have further evidence from Arab American respondents that broad abstract ideologies about cultural diversity translate directly into the desire for concrete steps to be taken to maintain ethnic cultures and language, one's own as well as those of other ethnolinguistic groups. (p. 64)

Since language and culture appear to be the most important aspects of heritage, they remain the main variables used to study the acculturation processes of Arabic students.

Indeed, linguistic and cultural elements often unite Arabs and Arab Americans together, and it takes on an added significance after considering the significant wave of Arab immigration into the United States. According to the Detroit Free Press's web article, "100 Questions and Answers about Arab Americans," the first major influx of Arab emigration into the U.S. began in 1875, lasting until 1920, bringing with it individuals searching for financial opportunities. Banks (1981) explains that the "outbreak of the Great War in Europe in 1914 greatly increased the suspicion and distrust of immigrant groups in the United States" (p. 3), consequently fueling the dominant culture's need to assimilate its immigrant populations into mainstream society.

The second wave of immigration, beginning in 1940, was a direct result of the Arab-Israeli conflict and civil war. The website also notes that the second group of immigrants had more individuals practicing Islam, a religion not well known in the United States during that time. Before this period, most Arab immigrants arriving into America were Christian, but Feagin and Booher (2003) reveal that "since the 1960s most Arab immigrants have been Muslim," stating that "there were at least 52 mosques in the United States" (p. 335). This second influx of settlers usually had more financial security upon arrival into the U.S. than the first group did as well, seeking better educational opportunities while in the America.

"100 Questions and Answers about Arab Americans" explains that the United States has dealt with these Arab immigrants by classifying them as African, Asian, White, European, or a separate group. Indeed, the U.S. government does not classify the Arab population by race or list them as a minority group because of employment and housing purposes. Unlike some minorities, Arabs are not defined by race. Indeed, the United States Census Bureau does list Arab as a separate race. Consequently, they unite themselves by cultural and linguistic similarities instead Although, the web article continues, noting that some Arab Americans see minority classification as a necessity for full participation in American life, and despite the dual loyalties that many Arab Americans feel between the United States and their countries of origin, most Arab Americans were born in the United States and possess U.S. citizenship.

As citizens of the United States, the web article explains that Arab Americans are represented in a wide variety of occupational types: business, medicine, education, and the sciences. More likely than not, they are self-employed or work in sales, and according to the website, roughly 60% of working Arab Americans are executives, professionals, or office and sales staff; at the local level, Arab Americans are most apt to hold executive positions in Washington, D.C. or Anaheim, California and manufacturing occupations in Detroit, Michigan. As with most people, though, "100 Questions and Answers about Arab Americans" concludes that employment choices are often influenced by an individual's nationality, religion, education, socio-economic status, and/or gender.

As a Palestinian, I have seen first-hand the influence that one's nationality which is the belonging to Arab World and native country of the individual, plays in an individual's life; the hijab, or head-scarf, illustrates my observations. I grew up around women who covered their heads; this is a religious and cultural practice, one rooted in the Islamic teachings of hijab, or modesty. While some say that veiling denigrates women, others say that it liberates them. The controversy surrounding this issue arises because covering is not universally observed by the Muslim religion, varying between different regions and classes explained in "100 Questions and Answers about Arab Americans". According to the website, islam.com (2000), an American mother or daughter may cover her head while others do not, and in Iraq and

Saudi Arabia, a woman may wear a cloak to cover her head and don traditional dress, causal clothes, or a business suit underneath her robe. In other words, each region's culture dictates the social mores concerning dress, and the hijab, in particular, has garnered controversy because of governmental policies, gender politics, and religious biases.

Another example illustrating how nationality can determine cultural mores deals with the social interactions between men and women. Islam.com explains Islamic behavior principles that some Arab men or women decline to shake hands with the opposite gender, and a number of Muslim males of Arabic descent, for religious purposes, avoid physical contact with women other than their close relatives (vice versa for some women). Although this is true for some, the website qualifies that this is not the case for all Muslims, noting that exceptions are made to help women who require assistance to cross the street, need help with an injury, etc.

Despite the differences that nationality, class and economy imprint on individual lives, most Arab countries are predominantly Muslim. However, most Muslims are not Arabs, a fact observed by islam.com, noting that roughly 12% of Muslims are Arab. Indeed, it explains that there are more Muslims in Indonesia than in the Arab countries. Harris and Moran (1996) explain, though, that "the waves of immigration into the area [Middle East] for thousands of years, have extended from the first Sumerians possibly from Central Asia to the latest Filipino or Indian migrant in search of work" (p. 342). Thus, although most Arab countries are Muslim, Harris and Moran (1996) note that "the Middle East has been marked by *diversity*" (p. 342).

The website islam.com (2000). explains that the Quran is the Muslim holy book, a work containing the word of God. The Quran was a message reveled to the prophet Mohammad, and it contains passages similar to those found in the Bible, another book regarded as holy. Originally, the Quran was written in Arabic, but it has been translated into different languages, including English. Harris and Moran (1996) state that "the Koran contains the discourse of Allah revealed to his prophet Muhammad. Yet as a religion, Islam has diversity in terms of different interpretations of its teachings by Sunni Muslims . . . or the Shi'ites Muslims" (p. 344).

Despite the diversification of Muslims, islam.com explains that the holiest Islamic sites are in the Middle East, and Arabic Muslims, whether in the United States or outside of the country, face Mecca, one of the three holy cities located in Arabia, to pray; Saudi Arabia's Medina and Jerusalem are the other two sites, and Ramadan, the ninth month of the Arabic Muslim calendar (354 days based on cycles of the moon), is a fasting month, a time of self-discipline and purification. Throughout its duration, Muslims abstain from food, drink, or sex during the period between sunup and sundown. Since the Islamic calendar is based on the cycles of the moon, Ramadan does not necessarily occur during the same time of the year, but for the Arabic Muslims, it is the most important Islamic observance of each year, ending with the celebration of Eid al-Fitr. Another major celebration that Muslims observe is Eid al-Adha on the last day of the hajj—the pilgrimage to Mecca.

**Background of the Arab World**

Palestine, Jordan, Lebanon, and Syria comprise the Arab speaking states of the eastern Mediterranean Sea. The Arabian Gulf countries are Saudi Arabia, Oman, Qatar, Kuwait, Iraq, Yemen, Bahrain, and the United Arab Emirates. The northern part of Africa, Egypt, Sudan, and Somalia and North-western African Morocco, Mauritania, Libya, Algeria, and Tunisia make up the rest of the Arab world. The Middle Eastern lands (Appendix A) occupy a unique geographical position, lying between and linking the three continents of the Old World. Therefore, it is expected that cultural influences from all three continents are strongly represented. Although many people believe that Arabic people share a common and standardized language and religion, one can readily find individuals living in this part of the world who do not speak a standard Arabic vernacular. Despite this difference, Patai (2002) explains that "when the inhabitants of two or more countries speak the same language, the common tongue constitutes a bond among them, an affinity and a sympathy that transcends divisive political boundaries" (p. 43). While Islam is the major religion in the areas described above, there are those who practice Christianity and Judaism as well, and though this population is of mixed ethnicity, practicing different religions, and ways of life, the Arab world is nonetheless united by its language.

Fisher (1987) describes the area climatically:

One basic reason for the distinctive character of the Middle East and North Africa is the special and unusual climate. Most parts of the world experience their rainfall either mostly during summer (the warm season) or distributed throughout the year. Only in a very few areas is there a maximum in winter (the cold season). This is the so-called 'Mediterranean' climate, giving a long intensely hot summer, and a relatively mild, rainy winter, with occasional cold spells. The distinction may not seem very important, but it conditions plant life to a remarkable degree, and thus also agriculture and general ways of life. Native plants rest in the hot season, not in the cold one, which is the opposite of what happens in cooler temperate climates. Some indigenous plants, such as cereals, mature quickly in order to complete a rapid growth cycle before the onset of hot weather; others, chiefly bulbs, flower in spring or autumn. (p. 6)

Patai (1969) explains why the Occident has interests in the Middle East, specifically the Arab world, stating that

> Advantageous geographical position, rich natural resources, a relatively dense population, successes in past history, and early independence are factors which made for a high rate of change, that is, a relatively . . . speedy and efficient "westernization," the outstanding example of which is Turkey itself. (p. 15)

Although the Middle East appeals to many Europeans and Americans, it has also been used to describe Arabs negatively; Feagin and Booher (2003) note that "since the 1960s, U.S. political and military policies regarding the Middle East have often generated or accelerated the spread of negative stereotypes" (p. 326). Indeed, the

> common labeling of Arab and other Middle Eastern peoples with terms such as "camel jockies" and "sand niggers" during the early 1990s' Gulf War and more recent Middle Eastern conflicts . . . helped to rationalize the conflicts in the minds of many non-Middle Eastern Americans. (Feagin & Booher, p. 326)

Consequently, this can lead to confusion between Arab and non-Arab Americans, a problem considering that "there are approximately 12 very large populations of Arabs scattered across the United States that are primarily concentrated in Michigan, Illinois, Ohio, California, New York, and Virginia" (Nassar-McMillan & Hakim-Larson, 2003). The United States Census Bureau does not racially designate a slot for the Arab culture, though; thus, it is difficult to ascertain their numbers according to these records.

**Arabic Language**

      I grew up speaking Arabic as a first language, and Arabic, like many other languages, possesses a beauty that influences millions of people around the world. Feagin and Booher (2003) estimate that more than 300 million people speak the Arabic language, making it the seventh most common language in the world. They continue by stating that it was the first language spoken by the people in the Middle East, and it is the language of Islam and the Quran, the Muslim holy book. Indeed, despite the importance that religion plays in unifying Arabs, language does so as well. According to the article, "All about the Arabic Language, 2002" found on the American Association of Teachers of Arabic website,

> Arabic is the language of a rich culture and civilization dating back many centuries; it was the language of Muhammad, the Messenger of God and Prophet of Islam, and the Qur'an . . . Between the eighth and the fifteenth centuries, the volume of literary, scholarly and scientific book production in Arabic and the level of urban literacy among readers of Arabic were the highest the world had ever known to that time. (¶ 1)

The piece continues, noting that over 160 million individuals speak Arabic in an area extending from the eastern Arabian Gulf to the western Atlantic ocean, explaining also that three million people within the United States and Canada speak the language; although a difficult tongue to master, the article posits that it is a rewarding one to learn, allowing individuals to apply it into their professional and academic pursuits, important because the United Nations adopted Arabic as one of its six official languages in 1976, thus ensuring its significance in world affairs.

Based on my own experiences with the Arabic culture, I know that Arabic is considered a Semitic language, and my study of sixth century Arabic literature has also taught me that the language was preserved through orally transmitted poetry. Indeed, during the earliest stages of Islam, Arabic was spread through both poetry and the Quran, transcripts written on leather, stone, and coins.

"All about the Arabic Language" also notes that the Quran was one of the earliest surviving documents of written Arabic, consequently reflecting the western dialect of Mecca; although, during the seventh century, scholars living in Lower Iraq imposed certain eastern dialectal features onto Arabic pronunciation, adding reading marks, but formal documents (inscriptions, tombstones, coins, etc) maintain the language found in the Quran, ignoring certain dialectal influences in the process. Indeed, I am aware of the differences between standard Arabic and its spoken dialects; standard Arabic is the language of all governmental establishments, such as schools, television stations, and the media, and it is the official language for all Arabic speaking countries.

Despite the universal use of Standard Arabic in its written format, "All about the Arabic Language" concedes that its spoken form differs dialectically between the various countries and towns; however, these disparities are not large enough to change its structural features or create dissimilar vocabularies. Indeed, the website notes that its uniform grammar and vocabulary create a potent symbol of Arab cultural and religious unity, significant considering it is the language of the Quran.

During one of my interviews with a school teacher, she noted how important language is as a source of cultural identity, proclaiming:

> I am hoping that the children will not lose their language and culture. I hope they can get it from the family or the family can get it for their children. I wish we had an educational system where we could offer more than English or Spanish. At this point, we are in the dark ages.

I feel that effective multicultural teachers must have a knowledge of the English and non-English languages in their classrooms, regardless of their teaching levels. Also, teachers should have an awareness of their students' languages, but at present, real school settings do not really acknowledge other languages, a fact noted by one third-grade teacher that I interviewed. She commented,

"We need more Arabic teachers to work with students in dual language programs," an idea expanded by a fourth-grade teacher's statement,

"I hope that a bilingual teacher can speak fluently in English and the native language of their students. I hope that the teachers teach in English as much as possible but with the native language to back up what is being taught in English."

Many of the interviewed teachers also thought that additional materials and resources were needed in the curriculums in order to create a multicultural environment that would address the language issues experienced by Arabic students. At present, the curriculum only provides for English or Spanish/English classrooms, something that one second-grade teacher hopes will soon cover the Arabic culture as well. She stated:

> We don't have any materials to enable me to read in their own language. We are very limited with what we have academically for them; we only have Spanish for Spanish-speaking students. Since the Arabic population is growing in the schools and community, something should be addressed by the administration.

Thus, in order to better include the Arabic student in the classroom, many teachers feel that the school systems must provide better training and more materials on how to best represent the Arabic culture in the educational sphere.

**Chapter Summary**

Cultural and linguistic traditions are important factors of the Arabic student's self-identity. In order to represent the Arabic voice in the United States School System, the Arabic language and culture must be represented in the school curriculum. Sonia Nieto (2002) explains that a

> major problem with a monocultural curriculum is that it gives students only one way of seeing the world . . . But to be informed and active participants in a democratic society, students need to understand the complexity of the world and the many perspectives involved. (p. 43)

Through this qualitative study, I revealed how the Arabic language and culture has not been adequately represented in the school systems of the United States. Consequently, I also argued the need for more multiculturalism in education, allowing the Arabic students and their families to gain a stronger voice in the school system as a result.

# CHAPTER 2

# LITERATURE REVIEW

**Acculturation**

The acculturation theory for this qualitative study of Arab American is the single–continuum model of acculturation, and it is described as the changing of an ethnic traditional cultural trait for an Anglo cultural traits. For Ponterotto (2001) the exchange of cultural traits results in becoming more like the Anglo culture, and it is represented as a point on a continuum ranging from being unacculturated, bicultural, to acculturated. The process of acculturation is developed in three stages, which result in a direct effect on the adopted person. These stages include contact, conflict and adaptation (p.394-421).

Although the concept lacks a theoretically grounded distinction in literature, early models of acculturation were similar to those of assimilation Traditionally, theorists viewed acculturation as a linear process, one where the individual accommodated to the host culture by abandoning her/his native cultural values. Herskovits (1938) explains that Ehrenreich uses the term in reference to the "area of acculturation" and "acculturational relationships" (pp. 4-5). He likewise noted that in the 1928 version of Webster's Unabridged Dictionary, acculturation was defined as "the approximation of one human race or tribe to another in culture or arts by contact," later revised in the 1934 edition to read, "the approximation of one social group of people to another in culture or arts by contact; the transfer of cultural elements from one social group of people to another" (p. 2). For Herskovits (1938),

Lesser uses the term "acculturation" to denote a reciprocal relationship of give and take based on both cultures, where assimilation is the total adaptation of a ruling culture and is different than acculturation. Herskovits continues by citing an additional comment by Lesser, stating:

> Acculturation may be taken refer to the ways in which some cultural aspect is taken into a culture and adjusted and fitted to it. This implies some relative cultural equality between the giving and receiving cultures. Assimilation, however, is the process of transforming aspects of a conquered or engulfed culture into a status of relative adjustment to the form of ruling culture. The problem of acculturation, when we are considering the American Indians in relation to their adjustment to European culture, is a problem of assimilation (p. 7).

Although, Gordon (1964) contends that the concepts of assimilation and acculturation were of interchangeable usage, descriptions of an individual's transfer of identification from her/his original ethnicity or race to mainstream American society.

According to Herskovits (1938), early researchers used acculturation as a descriptive term, and it was defined once again for Herskovits in the 1936 edition of the New Standard Dictionary as "the imparting of culture by one people to another" (p. 2). Herskovits continues by describing the enormous effects that acculturation has had on different groups, citing Powell's 1880 statement that "The force of acculturation under the overwhelming presence of millions has wrought great changes" (p. 3). For Gordon (1964), acculturation is a "change of cultural patterns to those of the host society" (p. 71); followed by Vierkandt in 1908, the latest researchers have also devoted some attention to the phenomenon of acculturation, noting its significance in cultural dynamics. Cultural change occurs as a result of a number of processes (Spindler, 1977), ensuing from the contact of two or more different cultures. Acculturation, for Portilla (1990), is "the process of, or reciprocal consequences derived from, the coming together or contact of groups bearing different cultures" (p. 243), and the phenomenon of acculturation continues to attract the attention and interest of educational researchers.

However, it was not until the 1930s that acculturation was formally recognized as an area of scientific inquiry. In 1936, the Social Science Research Council (SSRC) appointed a Subcommittee on Acculturation consisting of Redfield, Linton, and Herkovits, three distinguished anthropologists, for the purpose of identifying and defining the parameters of acculturation (Portilla, 1990); Melville Herkovits (1938) explains that the SSRC "made possible a period of reflection and reading on the problems" associated with acculturation (p. iii), and consequently, he was able to determine that acculturation resulted when groups of culturally different individuals experienced continuous first-hand contact, subsequently changing the original cultural patterns of either or both groups. This definition is distinguished, for Herskovits, from culture-change, even while assimilation is, at times, a phase of acculturation, and such a definition provides a general view of the nature of cultural change.

The Social Science Research Council Summer Seminar on Acculturation (1954) formulated a definition of acculturation that delineates more specific characteristics of this process, providing another view of the cultural changes taking place in research paradigms:

> Culture change is initiated by the conjunction of two or more autonomous cultural systems. Acculturative change may be the consequence of direct cultural transmission; it may be derived from noncultural causes, such as ecological or demographic modifications induced by an impinging culture; it may be delayed, as with internal adjustments following upon the acceptance of alien traits or patterns; or it may be a reactive adaptation of traditional modes of life. Its dynamics can be seen as the selective adaptation of value systems, the processes of integration and differentiation, the generation of developmental sequences, and the operation of role determinants and personality factors. (p. 974)

A number of contemporary researchers have argued that the assimilation model characteristic of early research is not sufficient or satisfactory to explain the processes of acculturation. Dohrenwend and Smith (1962) hypothesize that acculturation involves two distinct and independent dimensions: the first being the retainment or the loss of traditional cultures, and in the second, new cultural traits are acquired, allowing individuals to acculturate without necessarily losing native cultural traits. Roysircar-Sodowsky and Maestas (2000) explain that "acculturation is generally viewed as a process of change that occurs as a consequence of a continuous, first-hand contact of two or more distinct cultural groups" (p. 135), a definition that closely mirrors Berry's interpretation of acculturation.

Berry (1980) describes the phenomenon of acculturation as multidimensional. First, it is a dimension that "requires the contact of at least two autonomous cultural groups; there must also be change in one or other of the two groups which result from contact" (p. 10). Berry delineates another dimension of acculturation by noting that it has a three-phase course of contact, conflict, and adaptation; contact is the interaction of two or more cultural groups, leading to the conflict that occurs when a group resists the domination of another one; this is where the reduction of conflict, or the third phase of acculturation, occurs.

This third stage, adaptation, has three distinct varieties: adjustment, reaction, and withdrawal. Adjustment occurs when the behaviors of one group become similar to those of a dominant group (homogenization, assimilation). Reaction occurs when a group challenges a dominant group through disagreement. Withdrawal happens when a group is isolated or alienated from the dominant one.

Berry (1980) also views acculturation as the adaptive processes of a non-dominant group to the pressures imposed by the dominant body. There are four types of adaptation that exist at either the group or individual levels. The first type is rejection, a withdrawal (self-segregated or forced) from the larger society. In the case of Chicanos, rejection of North American culture involves not participating in or being allowed to participate in this culture.

The second type is adjustment or assimilation; it includes accepting a cultural identity and adopting the trends and identities of the dominant culture. Assimilation has two varieties, commonly known as the "melting Pot" or the "pressure cooker." The "melting pot" occurs when groups choose to move freely to the larger group (internal processes), and the "pressure cooker" (Anglo-conformity ideology) develops when groups are forced to move into larger societal models (external processes).

The third type of adaptation is integration, or the attempt to become a part of the dominant society while trying to maintain the identification values of one's native culture. Integration requires that the host society value a pluralistic or multicultural society, mainly because assimilation cannot be successful without the host society's acceptance.

The final type of adaptation is de-culturation, a process resulting from the loss of both values of identification: an individual is alienated from the dominant culture and her/his culture of origin; when de-culturation is imposed by the host society, ethnocide is a consequence. In order to keep this instance from occurring, many Arab Americans attempt to retain their Middle Eastern culture while also assimilating into North American society. Feagin and Booher (2003) explain that "while almost half of Arab Americans over the age of seventeen speak some language beside English in their homes, . . . in most homes two languages [English and Arabic] are the norm" (p. 337). Thus, most Arab Americans, though assimilating into the predominant culture of the United States, still hold onto their Middle Eastern heritages.

The broad definition of acculturation has resulted in three models of acculturation. First, the single–continuum model of acculturation is described as the changing of an ethnic traditional cultural trait for Anglo cultural traits. The exchange of cultural traits causes the individual to become more like the Anglo culture, and it is represented as a point on a continuum ranging from being unacculturated, bicultural, to acculturated (Ponterott, 2001). The second way of conceptualizating acculturation is the two-culture matrix model. This model describes two cultures being two separate continuums where individuals accept different parts of each other. The person can be unacculturated, bicultural, marginal or acculturated. The third model of acculturation is the multidimensional model. In this model a person may exchange a traditional cultural trait for a new one and still maintain many of the native traits.

For Gordon (1964), the assimilation that many cultures, including Arab Americans, experience while in the United States consist of seven isolated sub processes:

1. Cultural assimilation or acculturation: change of cultural patterns to those of the host society.
2. Structural assimilation: large-scale entrance into cliques, clubs, and institutions of the host society.
3. Marital assimilation (amalgamation): large-scale intermarriages.
4. Identification assimilation: the development of a sense of citizenship based on the host society.
5. Attitude receptional assimilation: the absence of prejudice.
6. Behavior receptional assimilation: absence of discrimination.
7. Civic assimilation: Absence of value and power conflict.

The first three points are considered the fundamental aspects of assimilation, and cultural assimilation can be either external or internal behaviors, characterized by a distinctive institutional life within sub-societies like clubs and churches. Structural assimilation is the large-scale entrance into cliques, clubs, group activities, or home visits of the host society on primary relations. Marital assimilation has deep effects on future generations of the ethnic minorities; with intermarriages come problems of marginality, an occurrence which prevents the children from finding acceptance from either the dominant or the non-dominant cultures. Also, marriages of mixed religions often end in divorce or conversion on the part of one spouse from her/his native religion.

Following the same model, Warner and Srole (1945) introduce cultural types in order of potential assimilation, a list that reads:

1. The English-speaking Protestants.
2. Protestants who do not speak English.
3. English-speaking Catholics and other non-Protestants.
4. Catholics and other non-Protestants, most of whom speak allied Indo-European languages.
5. English-speaking non-Christians.
6. Non-Christians who do not speak English.

For most Arab Americans, they fall under either the fifth or the sixth sections. Indeed, English is often a second language, and most Arab Americans are non-Christian, instead practicing Islam. Thus, they have a much more difficult time assimilating and acculturating into United States society because their cultural values are different from the majority of American citizens.

Acculturation, as a field of study, is considered an interdisciplinary perspective, related directly to anthropology, sociology, and psychology. Padilla (1980) relates acculturation to psychological perspectives on cultural change within the individuals. Sociologists and psychologists were first interested in acculturation and assimilation as a way to study the group processes of minority groups and race relations (Gordon, 1964). While anthropologists and psychologists studied acculturation as a group process, psychologists focused on the individual experience in the process of acculturation. In psychological studies focused primarily on European ethnicity, psychological researchers paid more attention to the study of the individual's language, cognitive style, personality, identity, attitudes, and acculturation stress (Olmedo, 1979).

Only later did the focus shift to the study of minorities. This increasing shift toward the individual as the unit of analysis has prompted psychology to become more involved in acculturation research (Olmedo, 1979). Consequently, different acculturation models have developed to study minorities, both individually and in groups. These models focus on the direction and dimension of acculturation that minority groups experience when adapting to a dominant society.

**Acculturation Models**

The single-continuum model is the base of this qualitative study, and the directional nature of acculturation proposes that the direction is dependent on the context within which the individual is acculturated (Szapocznik & Kurtines, 1980). This directional model, based on studies of Cuban immigrants in Miami, hypothesizes that acculturation may be unidirectional (single continuum), bi-directional (two-culture matrix), or multidirectional depending on the cultural context, and if the total context is mono-cultural, the acculturation processes will tend to be linear, unidirectional, and assimilative in nature. An example of this situation occurs when individuals emigrate to monolingual communities: the acculturation processes of these individuals will involve learning the monolingual culture, thus abandoning all characteristics of their native cultures. "According to this theoretical model," Szopocznik and Kurtines (1980) posit, the "individual acculturation is a linear function of the amount of time a person has been exposed to the host culture, and of the rate at which acculturation process takes place is a function of the age and sex of the individual" (p. 141). Thus, second-generation Arab Americans are often more acculturated to American customs and fluent in the English language than their parents because they are exposed to these within the public school system.

Recent investigators view acculturation as a multidimensional process involving various cultural dimensions (Olmedo, 1979). When the total context is bi-cultural, the acculturation process is this way as well, and individuals can acculturate by simultaneously accommodating to the host culture while retaining their own heritages. Richard Bucher (1999) explains that assimilating into the dominant culture involves "the process in which people lose their cultural differences and blend into the wider society" (p. 10), but he also contends that not all of the minority groups assimilate completely into the prevailing culture. Instead, they do it up to a point or do not assimilate at all. Despite the multidimensional nature of acculturation promoted by researchers like Bucher, though, there are others who see it mono-dimensionally.

Although theorists disagree about what constitutes the dimensions of acculturation, investigators do recognize that individuals acculturate differently along each dimension. Moore and Pachon (1985) note that there is general agreement among researchers that language familiarity and usage, interactions with fellow minorities, cultural awareness, ethnic loyalty and identity, and generational proximity are the important dimensions involved in the processes of acculturation. For Zintz (1969), acculturation occurs in consequence of the interactions between cultural groups of unequal strength, one dominant and the other subordinate, leading more minority group members to culturally identify both socially and economically with the dominant model. This is due to the dominant group's control of the economic base, public health-care programs, and educational policies. Consequently, many Arab Americans, though maintaining some of their cultural heritages, must assimilate into mainstream American society for economic, health and education purposes.

Historically, school socialization processes were the primary ways for children to learn normative values. Indeed, North American public schools are important social institutions, places where children are socialized, learning essential functions for socio-economic development in the process (Mohl, 1991). If all cognitive work is done using a dominant language, the amount of exposure to this language becomes another way that the dominant culture, through education, has minorities learn and participate in English-only learning environments, thus enacting and reproducing cultural norms. Mohl (1991) states:

> It is only within the framework of the schools' socialization functions that we can fully and properly understand the history of minority education in the United States. Ethnic and racial minorities came to the schools with different languages, cultures, traditions, and values. For the maintenance of social order and cohesion, the socialization and assimilation of these minority groups was thought to be doubly important. As a homogenizing agent, as an

> institution designed to secure conformity to the American way, the public schools thus took on the special task of breaking down and destroying ethnic and racial cultures. For minority groups—European and other immigrants, American Indians, Chicanos, and Blacks—socialization in the public schools meant a vigorous effort to wipe out the old culture and to propagate the new. (p. 188)

Since the turn of the twentieth century, educational programs were developed to meet the needs of a dominant group, thus ensuring that the public schools have become the centers for assimilation processes. If all educational programs aim to "cook" ethnic minorities into one dominant culture, using a single language, English, while ascribing to capitalistic values, the inclusion of individuals from all minority groups is necessary (Mohl, 1991).

Feagin and Booher (2003) comment on the way Arab Americans are assimilated into the United States Public School System, describing an instance where "one Arab American educator recently noted that non-Arab teachers often fail to realize that not all Arab Americans share the same cultural background" (p. 334). They continue by indicating that educators need to "become more sensitive to the major cultural practices of Arab Americans, such as respecting major Arabic holidays, and to become better informed about Middle Eastern history and contemporary political issues" (p. 334). Otherwise, Mohl (1991) suggests, it cannot be said that the North American public schools offer equal opportunities for all social groups. Instead, stereotyping of minority groups like Arab Americans can occur, mainly because most students are not educated about the culture and values of these groups and often have inaccurate ideas about them.

In the acculturation process, we cannot ignore the gender, stereotype, prejudice, and discrimination issues of different cultures. The differences that could differentiate males from females vary from culture to culture. For example, Haneef (2000, p. 165) explains that within the Arabic culture there are a lot of differences between males and females, from dress codes to social mixing, behaviors in speaking, to physical appearance. Within the Arabic culture, these patterns are initiated from the Islamic teachings of modesty. Theses pattern are different for males and females within the circle of family and within the outside public. It is worth mentioning the effects that stereotyping has on people when we lump them into a category and assume that they all are alike. For Bucher (2004, p. 82) stereotypes can lead to prejudice because exposure to rigid images of a particular group can lead individuals to have preconceived images of anyone in that particular group. In the process of acculturation, prejudice leads to unequal treatment (discrimination) of different groups in our society based on their group membership because of race, gender, age, or social class (Bucher, 2004, p. 91).

**Stereotyping**

Through my interviews with the Arabic children and their families, I discovered that many of students had received some form of stereotypical slur against them while attending public school. Some of the stereotypes that they mentioned were found in their school textbooks; Griswold (1975) notes that in 1971, the Middle East Studies Association, or "Image Committee," conducted research detailing how various secondary school textbooks included stereotypical depictions of the Middle Eastern or Arabic worlds into their information, consequently enabling North American biases to receive precedence. Indeed, this study evaluated Canadian and North American images in secondary geography and history textbooks, demonstrating that the textbook authors lacked the scholarly background necessary for specialized knowledge about the Middle East, information that textbooks were espousing as standardized truth. The study also revealed the necessity for teachers to become aware of possible biases in their own views of the Middle East.

Indeed, some North American authors hold cultural biases regarding the ethnicity of Arabic people, and a number of their textbooks depict a colorful life in the desert regions, painting a nomadic Arabic culture where its people wear colorful clothes with Kaffiyeh and ride camels. Secondary world history and social studies texts generally demonstrate high standards of geographical and cartographical accuracy, representing correctly defined geo-political boundaries, but at the same time, they ignore the large number of urbanized, middle-class Arabs living in large cities like Beirut or Cairo. Such stereotyping practices are often supported by photographs depicting Arabs as either Bedouins or millionaires.

Griswold (1975) continues by noting that the biases often present themselves in school materials; for instance, very few texts describe the Arab century of expansion under the Umayyad caliphs. Indeed, many of these texts ignore the seventh-century Caliphate, instead beginning with a more colorful account of the Abbasids in ninth-century Baghdad. Griswold (1975) explains that one misleading stereotype of the Arabic culture concerns Saladin, mainly because a number of the texts report that "he was a 'good' Muslim, and thoughtful of his enemies, while other Muslims were 'conquerors'" (p. 12). One text even describes him as a "Sultan of the Turks," a grossly inaccurate fact; he was a Kurd hero (p. 12).

The religion of Islam is treated differently than Judaism or Christianity, the two previously established Semitic religions. Texts still describe Islam with misleading terms like, "the Mohammedan Religion" (Griswold, 1975, p. 17), deeming that Islam is the religion of the typical desert Arab, ignoring the millions of non-Arabic Muslims in the process. Emphasizing the misinterpretation of Muslim behavior in secondary texts, Griswold (1975) cites how one book states, "A Moslem priest might write a Koran verse on paper, wipe off the ink, and have the patient drink the ink and water as medicine" (p. 17), failing to clarify this practice. Griswold also illustrates how textbooks often call a student's attention to a masculine heaven, maintaining that Muslim women have culturally inferior statuses.

Shaheen (2000) explains that Hollywood continues to play a role in the demonizaton of the Arabic culture. Indeed, Arabs are often characterized as stupid, sexy, oily Sheiks, blood-loving fanatical terrorists, or backward Bedouins. For example, Palestinians are portrayed as religious radicals, something that Shaheen notes, stating:

> Palestinians are characterized by Hollywood as religious fanatics, threatening our freedom, economy, and culture. Producers portray Palestinians as a demonic creature without compassion for men, women or children. Palestinian Muslim images reflect a combination of past stereotypes, such as those which depict Hispanics as "wet backs," Jews as insurgents, blacks as sexual predators, Asians as sneaky, and American Indians as "savages." The

"Palestinian equal terrorists" narrative surfaced in 1960, in Otto Preminger's Exodus. In the 1980s ten features, including The Ambassador (1984), The Delta Force (1986), Wanted Dead or Alive (1987), and Ministry of Vengeance (1989), put into effect images showing the Palestinian Muslim as Enemy Number One. Feature films tag him as "scumbag," "son of bitch." Several made-for-television movies also paint the Palestinian as a despicable being, including TV movies such as Hostage Flight (1985), Terrorist On Trial (1988), Voyage of Terror (1990), and Cinemax's 1989 documentary, Suicide Bombers Secrets of Shaheed. (p. 25)

**Theoretical Frameworks**

In the following, I will introduce some critical pedagogy patterns that will prove beneficial in improving curriculum, mainly because my study deals with the linguistic and cultural acculturating processes of Arabic students in the public school systems. Multiculturalism (Nieto, 2000), the Frankfurt school of critical theory (Stirk, 2000), and the Freirean approach (Freire, 1993) all present ways in which the curriculum can better include minority groups within the public school systems.

Banks (1996) explains that there is an important distinction between multiethnic education and multicultural education, stating that multiethnic education focuses on ethnic and racial groups and multicultural education concentrates on race, class, and gender. Thus, multicultural education umbrellas more people, and Sonia Nieto (2000) contends that "curriculum and materials represent the *content* of multicultural education, but multicultural education is above all a *process*" (p. 315). Indeed, Nieto realizes that the multiculturalism must adapt to the cultural changes of minority groups, including different perspectives in the process, and she sees it as a critical pedagogy.

Indeed, Appelbaum (2002) explains that critical multicultural education is a "critical pedagogy approach . . . that signals how questions of audience, voice, power, and evaluation actively work to construct particular relationships between teachers and students, institutions and society, and classrooms and communities" (p. 173). He continues by noting that critical pedagogy is an "approach to teaching and learning that takes as a central concern the issue of power in the teaching and learning context, and focuses on how and in whose interests knowledge is produced and transmitted" (p. 179). Thus, critical pedagogy is a pedagogy "that illuminates the relationships among knowledge, authority, and power, toward emancipation or liberation" (Appelbaum, 2002, p. 180).

Through classroom observations and teachers' interviews, my study on the acculturation of Arabic students concluded that there was little knowledge about the Arabic culture and language in the public school system. One reason for this was because its curriculum often ignored the Arabic heritage. Trumbull, et al. (2001) indicates that one way to represent the different perspectives of minority groups, such as Arab Americans, in the United States Public School System is to "revise curricula and textbooks thoroughly to be more representative of the histories and traditions of groups that make up U.S. society" (p. 23). Trumbull, et al. continues by stating, "some curricula . . . characterized as "anti-racist" are directed at raising teachers' and students' awareness of how textbooks and schools' institutional practices promote unconscious racism" (p. 23).

Feagin and Booher (2003) expand on this idea, noting that

> because prejudice against Arab Americans increases when political events involve Arabs, or are even speculated to involve them, educators need to be prepared to respond to possible harassment of Arab American students resulting from negative news reporting, and to invoke school policies against hate crimes and discrimination as appropriate. (p. 334)

Feagin and Booher advocate for multicultural education by encouraging teachers to present their students with diverse perspectives of the world. They ask that teachers include minority viewpoints in their lectures, especially if that group is being stereotyped because of world affairs.

For instance, Feagin and Booher note how during the Gulf War in the early 1990s, many U.S. citizens of Middle Eastern origin were labeled as "sand niggers" or "camel jockies" (p. 326), and Edward Said (as cited in Feagin and Booher) "described these generally negative and stereotyped views of Middle Eastern peoples as an ideology of *Orientalism*." For Said, *Orientalism* went "back some centuries in Western thought, pervading much scholarly work as well as popular thinking" (Feagin & Booher, 2003, p. 326). Multiculturalism attempts to examine and change these ideologies, allowing students to see how unfounded these stereotypes are by presenting them with a different perspective on their Arabic classmates.

Like multiculturalism, the theorists of the Frankfurt School (Stirk, 2000), an establishment founded in 1923 by a group of German theorists belonging to the Institute of Social Research, committed themselves to go beyond appearances and expose the social relations behind these images; in so doing, they hoped to develop a method of theory and critique that would shatter the existing structure of domination, attempting to account for Marx's failed predictions concerning the proletariat revolution in the process. Stirk (2000) explains that "the label, the Frankfurt School, came later and was initially used by others as a convenient shorthand to identify the advocates of critical theory" (p. 1).

Indeed, critical theory is considered an approach of study that looks at schools and societies in order to improve the educational system, aiming to critique and transform the political, social, cultural, and economical structures that constrain and exploit humankind (Freire, 1993). As such, it emphasizes the need to create a strategy that can question the construction of knowledge, providing individuals with new insights into the social constructions of knowledge. In order to portray as accurately as possible the Arabic culture, students, teachers, and parents must question the information presented about the Arabic culture, voicing their concern when they feel that it is stereotypically represented in the classroom.

As a part of this project, critical theory emphasizes the importance of curricula in the educational process, rejecting the passivity of hidden or official curricula in schooling, consequently arguing that a critical consciousness is necessary in the development of a transitive critical consciousness (Freire, 1993). As a way for people to recognize the validity of their opinions, construct their own senses of reality, and reject the domination of others, critical consciousness challenges and transforms critical dialogues and experiences to avoid the danger of "massification," and Freire (1993) notes that part of the socialization process is dialogic thinking, one that doesn't separate theory from practice; indeed, dialogue has an emancipatory role.

Thus, it is important for Arabic students to create dialogues between their teachers/peers and themselves, voicing when they feel that they are being misrepresented. Through this, they may change the perceptions that their teachers and classmates have about the Arabic culture.

Freire (1993) continues, noting that critical pedagogy views education as political, mainly because knowledge is not neutral. Indeed, critical pedagogy argues against the "banking concept," one that views students and teachers as nothing more than "passive receptacles" reinforcing the prevailing hegemony that causes teachers to work within the confines of a curriculum enforced by the educational administrative authority. Instead, critical pedagogy calls for the radical departure from educational models like the "banking concept," mainly because it leads to an internal struggle for duality among students and teachers. As a solution to the problems of limited democracy in the school systems, critical pedagogy encourages problem-solving, a process allowing both Arabic and non-Arabic students to develop the power to criticize their worlds, one that is dependent on a certain critical consciousness.

Critical educators using problem-posing techniques ask provoking questions, allowing students to pose their own critical questions to authority figures, consequently generating a mutual knowledge between them; this improves a student's capacity for verbal exchange, one that reveals her/his take on reality and criticism of traditional curriculum. Since the learning process cannot extrapolate itself from the political sphere, critical pedagogy also has students pose questions about their schools and society.

For Friere (1993), the educational curriculum had generative words and themes, thus creating the basis for reading, writing, and conversational activities, and through this, teachers became agents of change, teaching students how to be humanistic in a democratic society, a place where peace and equality should exist.

In order to promote a student-centered learning environment, the generative words and themes must derive themselves from a student's specific life-history or circumstance, allowing her/him to begin with encoding/decoding exercises that end with more complex tasks of transforming the world, a humanizing process used to affect action and obtain a critical consciousness. Freire (1993) notes that all of these activities are geared toward reaching a stage of conscientization, a method dealing against limit-situations and fatalism. Indeed, critical pedagogy is opposed to limit-situations and fatalism, modes disallowing students to objectively look beyond the false consciousness of a dominant society, constraining their ability to criticize the world through shared experiences in the process. Thus, this allows public school students to look beyond the "false consciousness" of the dominant society to see that many of the stereotypes of Arab Americans are unfounded.

Freire's language of possibility and hope requires students to actively participate in struggles for emancipation and empowerment, and I deeply believe that this language of hope renews the optimism and courage that changes both teachers and students. Indeed, one of the results of a liberal pedagogy is empowerment; it is a way to change our educational environments and realities, and Freire calls for praxis, something at the core of liberal education, in order to grant students power from the learning processes. As students familiarize themselves with these learning processes, creating their own form consciousness through self-determination, creativity, and rationality, an education of empowerment emerges from their collective actions. Thus, praxis works against coercion, homogeneity, and chance, allowing students to live with the world, not in the world.

"Mystification," on the other hand, is the process of alienation, oppressing a culture into disguising itself, thus creating false and naive interpretations of that culture, decreasing, as Freire believes, the likelihood of a critical consciousness in the process. Freire (1993) posits that participatory research, a process used by the oppressed to change and resolve their exploitation, is thus important. Indeed, by attaining knowledge, the oppressed can work toward achieving social equality, and Freire believes that collegiality, or the participation of members through consensual governance, is a characteristic of democracy; by involving themselves in decision-making, the oppressed acquire voices, breaking down the culture of silence, something that minority students do by sharing and receiving validation for their life-experiences, consequently helping form a group consensus.

Although Freire's (1993) critical philosophy has helped minority students acquire voices in mainstream society, it is also attacked as utopian. I agree that Freire's utopian notion is not idealistic, but his denouncement of dehumanization and his incorporation of more humanistic approaches offer an organic approach (living with the world, not in the world) to minority acculturation. For Freire, utopia is a planned project, one where people work to fulfill a plan, and the amount of time that it takes to implement this plan is one where individuals can construct their own realities.

**Chapter Summary**

Theorists, though not unanimous on the definitions of assimilation and acculturation, agree that some sort of measured action toward improving educational depictions of minority groups like Arab Americans must materialize; they feel that the subjugation of any group by a dominant one is detrimental to its growth and self-identity (Trumbull, et al.2001). Often times, stereotyping of minority groups form from the acculturation process because these groups' cultures are not well-represented in mainstream American society, allowing inaccurate depictions to take root in the public consciousness as a result (Feagin & Booher, 2003). Consequently, researchers like Freire and theories like multiculturalism have developed critical approaches to address these inaccurate depictions of minority groups in the United States Public School System. Through these approaches, Arabic students will hopefully have an outlet where they can accurately portray their linguistic and cultural heritages to their peers and teachers.

# CHAPTER 3

# METHODOLOGY

**Naturalistic Paradigm of Research**

Informally, I understand "paradigm" to mean a pattern or a set of individual beliefs. For Guba and Lincoln (1989), paradigms are belief systems based on Ontological, Epistemological, and Methodological assumption methods, also noting that a paradigm is a "basic set of beliefs, a set of assumptions we are willing to make, which serves as a touchstone in guiding our activities" (p. 80). In his description of scientific revolution, Kuhn (1970) refers to a paradigm as a creative ideology for producing knowledge.

A naturalistic paradigm is one of two paradigms of research; the other is a rationalistic one, a paradigm suitable for conducting studies in the "hard" sciences like chemistry and physics. My interests lie in the naturalistic paradigm, a model positing that reality is a social construction, and in this sense, it provides meaning to individuals about their lives (Denzin & Lincoln, 1998). I used the modified CIPP model when researching the Arabic children and their family members in the Arabic schools and homes in Pecan Valley, Green City, and Intermountain City. I also employed the model in the Pecan Valley and Intermountain City public schools.

A naturalistic paradigm seeks to study the reality of people in a holistic orientation, and by allowing for purposive sampling, it enables researchers to study in their natural settings (Rallis & Rossman, 1998). I like the idea of studying reality holistically because it provides a clearer interpretation of human behavior; research studies from a naturalistic paradigm enable researchers to participate with the phenomenon under study, emphasizing the importance of a researcher's subjectivity in the process (Uwe, 1998). Also, the naturalistic paradigm refers to the qualitative methodology of collecting meaningful data while using instruments in the research study.

**Evaluation versus Research**

Guba and Lincoln (1989) summarized history of evaluation during the past hundred years is one way to consider the implications that stereotyping and evaluating have on a group of people. It was from this background of evaluation that I modified the CIPP model of research. According to Guba, evaluation was used: in the first generation, as a measurement; the second generation, as a description; the third, judiciously; and the fourth, as a way to utilize the methodology of Constructivists. Guba (1989) explains that evaluation is an old phenomenon, dating back to 2000 BC when the Chinese used it to measure the proficiency of public schools. He also notes that Greek teachers, such as Socrates, used verbally mediated evaluation in the learning process.

Madaus, Scriven, and Stufflebeam (1983) describe six eras of evaluation; they explain that the first one, spanning between the nineteenth and twentieth centuries, was called the Era of Reform, mainly because it marked the time of industrial revolution and social change, both educationally and politically, in Great Britain and the United States. The second era, occurring between 1900-1930, was marked as the

Age of Efficiency and Testing, characterized by individual and group testing developments in educational and psychological decisions. The third era of evaluation, known as the Tylerian Age (1930-1945), was characterized by Ralph Tyler's (later known as the father of evaluation) continuation of the testing movement. Tyler conceptualized evaluation as a comparison of intended with actual outcomes, a study concentrating on the knowledge of expected outcomes instead of input data (outcome assessment).

The fourth era of evaluation occurred between 1946 and 1957, typified by poverty and despair, and it was known as the Age of Innocence in North American culture. Organizations like the American Psychological Association and the American Educational Research and National Council on Measurements established regulations on testing and achievements. Marked by racism and segregation, though, there was little effort to develop evaluation, and educational program evaluations were rare.

The fifth era of evaluation, characterized as the Age of Expansion, was most significantly marked in the field of education, allowing program evaluations to grow in all fields. One of the most influential educational evaluations was introduced by Congress's 1965 passage of the Elementary and Secondary Education Act (ESEA) in the United States. Enacted to allow state and local agencies to evaluate the effectiveness of Title I and Title II programs, ESEA was the first time that conceptualizations of the evaluative goals, criticism of inputs and implementations, program outcome assessments, and the object of study—the very criteria for study—

were evaluated separately. Stufflebeam (1983) explains that the CIPP model resulted in the late 1960s because of attempts to evaluate projects funded by the ESEA. There was a great demand to evaluate programs in order to include the minorities as a result from the Civil Right Movement in 1960s.

The CIPP model allowed agencies to improve their evaluation programs by utilizing four different types of evaluation (context, input, process, and product evaluation), and consequently, this helped decision-makers produce large amounts of information and outcome assessments. I used the CIPP model to study the acculturation of Arabic students in the public school systems because it allowed me to conduct a thorough investigation of the Arabic students' homes and the different schools' curricula concerning the Arabic language and culture.

During the sixth stage, the Age of Professionalism (1973-present), evaluation became a profession. In the 1970s, there was an increase in program evaluation quantity and budget size, something evidenced by the increase of federal support for program evaluations. This era saw the emergence of methodology textbooks and journals. At about this time, universities like UCLA, Boston College, Stanford University, University of Illinois, and University of Minnesota offered courses in evaluation methodology. The Joint Committee on Standards for Educational Evaluation (1981) developed the first principles and standards for program evaluations, guidelines followed in 1982 by a second set of standards issued by The Evaluation Research Society.

**Definition of Evaluation**

Berk (1981) introduces the first definition of evaluation, provided by Tyler in 1942 after his eight-year study at Ohio State University, as "the process of determining whether the objectives of a program have been achieved" (p. 4). Later educational theorists considered "evaluation" as a process by which data was gathered for the purpose of judgments and improvements to the system. Most of the current literature connects evaluation with the value of the things that are being evaluated. Bhola (1990) refers to evaluation "as the process of describing an evaluand [the entity being evaluated] and judging its merit and worth" (p. 10), and he mentions Stufflebeam's definition that described the process of delineating, obtaining, and providing useful information for alternative judgments in order to talk about evaluation. Bhola also uses George F. Madaus' definition: "an evaluation study is one that is designed and conducted to assist some audience to judge and improve the worth of some educational object" (p. 10). Worthen and Sanders (1987) define evaluation as "the determination of a thing's value. In education, it is the formal determination of the quality, effectiveness, or value of a program, product, project, process, objective, or curriculum" (p. 22). Evaluation is a complex process, but among theorists, there is no standard definition of educational evaluation.

**Evaluation Standards**

In 1981, the Joint Committee on Standards for Educational Evaluation Programs, Projects, and Materials (1994), established a list of guidelines for conducting evaluative studies, noting thirty standards summarized in four categories: utility, feasibility, propriety, and accuracy.

Utility standards concerned themselves with the following subclasses: audience identification, evaluator credibility, information and scope selection, evaluational interpretation and impact, report clarity, dissemination, and timeliness. Feasibility standards offered practical procedures that were both politically viable and cost effective. Propriety standards centered on topics like formal obligation, conflict of interest, full and frank disclosure, the public's right to know, human rights and interactions, balanced reporting, and fiscal responsibility. The fourth group of the standards, accuracy, deals with: object identification, or the clear identification of the evaluated subjects; context analysis, the description of the context of evaluation; and defensible information, which stipulates that sources are used, allowing for the information to be clearly described.

**Evaluation Models: CIPP as a Research Tool**

Bhola (1990) states that "a model is information, data or principles grouped, verbally or graphically to represent or describe a certain thing, idea, condition or phenomenon" (p. 27). In reviewing the literature about models, readers find numerous models for and types of evaluation. Bhola (1990) notes that there are a variety of evaluation models, including Tyler's Objectives-Oriented Model and Societal Experimentation Model, Robert E. Stake's Countenance of Evaluation and Responsive Evaluation, Malcolm Provus's Discrepancy Evaluation Model, Robert M.

Rippy's Transactional Model, Elliot W. Eisner's Evaluation as Connoisseurship Model, and Paulo Freire's Participatory Evaluation Model.

According to Stufflebeam (1983), "the CIPP model was conceptualized as a result of attempts to evaluate projects that had been funded through the Elementary and Secondary Education Act of 1965 (ESEA)" (p. 118). The original version of the CIPP model was developed by the Ohio State University Evaluation Center, created by the Phi Delta National Study Committee on Evaluation, and chaired by Daniel L. Stufflebeam (1971). The center was organized in 1965, helping agencies improve their evaluation programs by utilizing four different types of evaluations geared toward producing information and outcome assessments for decision-makers; these four types are: context, input, process, and product evaluation.

I was interested in using the CIPP Model for this study because I felt that it would enable me to conduct a thorough investigation of the students' homes and the different schools' curricula concerning the Arabic language and culture. The CIPP model is usually used quantitatively, but I used it as tool of investigation in my study of the acculturation of Arabic families and their children. I modify this model to meet my study investigation. The researchers get used to modify this model since 60s to meet their investigation purposes. Each of its four stages provides researchers with large amounts of information.

### Qualitative Procedures: CIPP Model of
### Evaluation as a Tool of Research

Stufflebeam developed the CIPP Model of Evaluation in the late 1960s, creating a tool to evaluate projects funded by the Elementary and Secondary Education Act of 1965. It was results of acknowledging minorities after Civil Right Movement in 1960s. Consequently, this model is mainly used quantitatively for program research. Indeed, the CIPP approach is based on the most important purpose of research, one that seeks to improve, not prove (Stufflebeam, 1983). The Ohio State University Evaluation Center first tested the CIPP Model, hoping to assist public schools and agencies, helping them improve their educational programs in the process. The center consequently helped other schools, institutions, and agencies to conduct a wide range of evaluations, and some of them used the tool qualitatively to research the acculturation processes of Arabic students; in order to study the acculturation of Arabic students in the Pecan Valley, Hot City, Green City, and Intermountain City school systems, the CIPP model (Table 1) completed a data collection, a process consisting of four types of research: contextual, input, process, and product research. As a mother of Arabic children, I was concerned about their educational futures, mainly because of the acculturation and assimilation issues facing Arabic children in the United States (U.S.). Indeed, there is a lack of knowledge in this country concerning the Arabic language and culture, something that must be addressed considering the growing number of Arabic students enrolling in the school systems.

For this qualitative study on the acculturation of Arabic students and their families in the United States, based upon my assumptions of the process of acculturation of Arab Americans, the following questions were used to research the Arabic students, their parents, and the teachers in the public school systems.

1. How much acculturation from a culture and a language point of view do Arabic students face in the public schools and nationwide?
2. What are some of the challenges Arabic students encounter in their schooling processes in the United States?
3. Do these difficulties change the parents', students', and teachers' learning environments?
4. Does ignoring the Arabic language and culture influence the parents and their children in the public schools?

In answering these questions, The CIPP model was used as a tool to study the target population. The four phases (Contextual, Input, Process, and product) of the model enrich my study by providing a huge amount of information about the target samples. The following stages will be the original model (Madaus, 1983) and my modification of the model to meet the needs of my research investigation on the acculturation of the Arabic families and their children in language and culture in the United States.

Contextual research (Madaus, 1983) objectives were to diagnoses the problems of a target population, leading to an assessment procedure bent on identifying curriculum weaknesses and strengths; contextual research defines a target population, assesses their linguistic and cultural needs, and attempts to diagnose the problems underlying these needs (Gredler, 1996), and contextual research allowed me to judge whether the proposed objectives (school curriculum) of schools were sufficient to meet Arabic students' cultural and linguistic needs. It also helped to understand acculturation process in language and culture of Arab American and to recommend future changes and recommendations for the target population.

In my qualitative study of acculturation, I interviewed the families at home and their children at home; I interviewed the students and their teachers at school. The contextual evaluation in the original model was done through different methodologies: survey, document review, hearings, interviews, diagnostic tests, and the Delphi technique (Madaus, 1983). In context of my study on the acculturation in language and culture for target populations, I used observation as a qualitative methodology to observe the language and culture in family homes and Arabic and public schools. Documentation was another source to look at, even though it was rarely available to the researcher. I also interviewed using the Seidman procedure for teachers (Appendix B), employed open-ended questions with students of middle and high school age (Appendix C), used Focus group interviews (Appendix D), interviewed to find out about the language preference of parents and their children (Appendix E), and interviewed to discover the cultural preference of students and their parents (Appendix F).

Input research in the original CIPP model was used to access system capabilities, alternative program strategies, procedural designs for implementing the strategies, budgets, and schedules (Stufflebeam, 1983). The methodology used in the original CIPP model for Input evaluation was discovered by inventorying and analyzing available human and material resources, solution strategies, procedural design for relevance, feasibility and economy, and by using such methods as literature research, visits to exemplary programs, advocate teams, and pilot trials (Stufflebeam, 1983).

Input research of language and culture in my study allowed me to identify implementation procedures for the purpose of proposing solution strategies, and this allowed me to identify the strategies, documentations, and procedural designs for implementation of language and culture in the future recommendations. In so doing, input research of language and culture helped me analyze the availability of human and material resources for Arabic students' needs, allowing me to plan and structure solution strategies and change activities as a basis for implementation for future recommendations.

In Input research of language and culture for my study of acculturation in language and culture of target populations, I used observation as a qualitative methodology to observe the language and culture in family homes, the Arabic school of Pecan Valley, and public schools. I interviewed teachers using the Seidman procedure (Appendix B), interviewed with open-ended questions with students of middle and high school age (Appendix C), used Focus group interviews (Appendix D), interviewed to find the language preference of parents and their children

(Appendix E), and interviewed to discover the cultural preference of students and their parents (Appendix F).

Process research objectives for the original model were to identify or predict in process, to discover defects in the procedural design or its implementation, to provide information for programmed decisions, and to record and judge procedural events and activities (Stufflebeam, 1983). The methodologies used in the original CIPP model of evaluation were of monitoring the activities and continuing interacting with and observing the activities of project staff (Stufflebeam, 1983).

Process research diagnoses procedural defects (Gredler, 1996), using this knowledge to refine the curriculum designs and procedures destined for implementation. Process research allowed me to research the negative side of implementing these designs; by observing the activities and projects in the classrooms, I identified procedural problems. In the process of researching the language and culture acculturation of target populations, I used observation as a qualitative methodology to observe the language and culture in the family homes, the Arabic school of Pecan Valley, and the public schools. Interviews with Seidman procedure for the teachers (Appendix B), Interviews with open-ended questions with students of middle and high schools (Appendix C), Focus group interviews (Appendix D), interviews of language preference with parents and their children (Appendix E), and interviews of cultural preference with students and their parents (Appendix F).

Product research objectives in the original model of CIPP were to collect descriptions and judgments of the outcomes and to relate them to objectives and to context, input, process information and to interpret their worth and merit. The methodologies for that were of defining operationally and measuring outcome criteria, by collecting judgments of outcomes and by performing qualitative and quantitative analysis (Stufflebeam, 1983). In my qualitative study of acculturation of Arabic families and their children in language and culture the product research, or summative research, collects all previous research and judgments in order to interpret their merit, collecting and judging all outcomes of contextual, input, and process research in the process (Hill, 1986). My study of product research also provided the opportunity to modify, refocus, and change the curriculum for future considerations of Arab American communities.

In my study, I used the CIPP model (Table 1) to observe the language and cultural preferences of students and parents in the Pecan Valley homes, conducted classroom observations at the Islamic Center of Pecan Valley, and interviewed teachers using the Seidman procedure (Appendix B) at the Pecan Valley Islamic Center and the Pecan Valley and Intermountain City public schools. I also interviewed and observed students in the Pecan Valley area using open-ended questions (Appendix C), interviewed the Pecan Valley focus groups (Table 2) using open-ended questions (Appendix D), and interviewed families in Hot City, Green City, and Intermountain City using open-ended questions (Appendices E & F).

Throughout the interviews that I conducted, I incorporated the research questions that were mentioned in chapter one. The list of questions read:

1. How much acculturation from a culture and language point of view do Arabic students face in the public schools and nationwide?
2. What are some of the challenges Arabic students encounter in their schooling processes in the United States?
3. Do these difficulties change the parents', students', and teachers' learning environments?
4. Does ignoring the Arabic language and culture influence the parents and their children in the public schools?

I used the CIPP model as a tool of research in my qualitative study on the acculturation processes of Arabic students at the Pecan Valley, Hot City, Green City, and Intermountain City public schools because I believe that this model plays an important role in understanding both the students and their families. Stufflebeam (1983) states,

> evaluation is also a necessary concomitant of improvement. We cannot make our programs better unless we know where they are weak and strong and unless we become aware of better means. We cannot be sure that our goals are worthy unless we can match them to the needs of the people they are intended to serve. (p. 140)

Also, it helps research school curriculum and improve it by allowing minority students to retain their cultural heritages, consequently increasing minority student participation and achievement (House, 1993).

Table 1
*CIPP Model*

| **CIPP Model of Research of Language and Culture** | *Settings* | *Qualitative Measurements* | **Type of Qualitative Measurement** |
|---|---|---|---|
| Contextual & Input Research at home of Language and Culture | Family Homes in Pecan Valley Area | Participant Observation | Home Observation of Language & culture |
| Contextual, Input, Process, and Product research | Arabic School in Islamic Center in Pecan Valley-Weekend Basis | Participant Observation, Interviews & Documentations | Classroom Observation & Teachers Interviews with Seidman procedure |
| Contextual, Input, Process, and Product research | Pecan Valley Public Schools | Teachers Interviews Documentation* | Teacher Interviews with Seidman Procedure |
| Contextual & Input at Home of language and Culture | Parents Interviews | Interviews & Observation | With Open-Ended Questions |
| Contextual & Input research at home of language and Culture | Children Interviews in Pecan Valley Area | Interviews & Observation | With Open-Ended Questions |
| Contextual &Input, Process and product of language and Culture. | Focus Group in Islamic Center in Pecan Valley Area | Interviews | Open-Ended Questions |
| Contextual &Input, Process and product of language and Culture | Arabic School in Islamic Center in Pecan Valley area; weekends only | Observation & Interviews | Seidmen Procedure |
| Contextual & input research of Language and Culture | Families Interviews in Hot City/TX (parents/children) | Interviews | Open-Ended Questions |
| Contextual & Input and product of Language and Culture at Home | Families Interviews in Green City (parents/children) | Interviews | Open-Ended Questions |
| Contextual & Input, process and Product of Language and Culture | Intermountain Public School (parents/children) | Teacher Interviews & Classroom observation | Seidman Procedure |
| Contextual &Input and Product of Language at home | Families Interviews in Intermountain City | Interviews | Open-Ended Questions |

**Table 2**
*Focus Group*

| Fathers | City Area | State | Country of Origin | Number of Children |
|---|---|---|---|---|
| Father #1 | Pecan Valley | NM | Jordan | 3 |
| Father #2 | Pecan Valley | NM | Kuwait [a] | 1 |
| Father #3 | Pecan Valley | NM | Yemen | 4 |
| Father #4 | Pecan Valley | NM | Iraq | 5 |
| Father #5 | Pecan Valley | NM | Jordan | 2 |
| Father #6 | Pecan Valley | NM | Jordan | 1 |
| Father #7 | Pecan Valley | NM | Jordan | 2 |
| Father #8 | Pecan Valley | NM | Saudi Arabia | 3 |
| Father #9 | Pecan Valley | NM | Jordan [a] | 2 |
| Father #10 | Pecan Valley | NM | Yemen | 3 |
| Father #11 | Pecan Valley | NM | Egypt [a] | 1 |
| Father #12 | Pecan Valley | NM | Algeria | 4 |
| Father #13 | Pecan Valley | NM | Yemen | 4 |
| Father #14 | Pecan Valley | NM | Jordan | 1 |
| Father #15 | Pecan Valley | NM | Palestine | 4 |

[a] Fathers not included in family sample

**The Setting**

My study on the linguistic and cultural acculturation of Arabic students and their families was conducted in different public school settings in Pecan Valley, New Mexico and Intermountain City, Utah; the study also occurred within the Islamic Center of Pecan Valley, a place where the families attended weekly meetings for the purpose of observation and interviewing. The students attended the Arabic school for two weekends during the fall and spring, and during the summer, were there on a daily basis. These students were of both genders males and females from different Arab countries. The parents decide to sent their children to Arabic school, because of their feeling that their language and culture been ignored though public education in public schools to a degree of loosing their language and culture. This school was established through Arabic families and run through teachers who their children are attending public schools. The parents are responsible for all the expenses and tuitions. In that case, the parents feel that this school will teach their children Arabic language and at the same way the children will be taught their cultural traditions. Besides the school setting, I also interviewed the students and their families in their homes, located in Hot City, Texas, Green City, New York, and Intermountain City, Utah (Table 3). In Hot City, I contacted the families through personal connections that I had made in Pecan Valley, New Mexico. Two families were agreeing to be interviewed, where I spent a day with each family for purpose of interviewing and observation of language and culture of home. In Green City, I knew the families that I was interviewing through personal friends, after several phone calls, I was able to interview five families within a two week visit to Green city, and in Intermountain City, I was personally connected to those families through college, I was able to interview three families living there.

**Table 3**
Settings

| Settings | Qualitative Measurements |
|---|---|
| Family Homes in Pecan Valley Area | Participant Observation |
| Arabic School in Islamic Center in Pecan Valley-Weekend Basis | Participant Observation, Interviews & Documentations |
| Pecan Valley Public Schools | Teachers Interviews Documentation* |
| Parents Interviews | Interviews & Observation |
| Children Interviews in Pecan Valley Area | Interviews & Observation |
| Focus Group in Islamic Center in Pecan Valley Area | Interviews |
| Arabic School in Islamic Center in Pecan Valley area; weekends only | Observation & Interviews |
| Families Interviews in Hot City/TX (parents/children) | Interviews |
| Families Interviews in Green City (parents/children) | Interviews |
| Intermountain Public School (parents/children) | Teacher Interviews & Classroom observation |
| Families Interviews in Intermountain City | Interviews |

**Population**

The population for this study, totaling twenty-five Arabic families, provided an in-depth understanding of the acculturation processes of Arabic students attending schools in Pecan Valley, New Mexico, Hot City, Texas, Green City, New York, and Intermountain City, Utah. Each family consisted of a father, a mother, and children from different school levels. Also, the study population included three principals from different elementary and high school levels, 14 teachers from all of the school levels, four tutors from the elementary levels, 50 Arabic parents, and 44 students of middle and high school age; the data was gathered from this study population by using interviews, family home observations, and class observations.

The families (Table 4) were contacted by phone in order to gain their permission to use them in this qualitative study, and I phoned some of the families in the Pecan Valley area because I knew them personally. I was introduced to the other families in the Pecan Valley area at the Islamic Center, and they contacted the families for me in order to get their permission to be researched.

In addition, I analyzed available schools documents, sources that were limited due to the lack of concern that Arabic children received despite their growing population within the school systems.

The selection of this population provides rich information for improving the curriculum to meet the linguistic and cultural needs of Arabic students, though, something that Denzin and Lincoln (1994) indicate when explaining that a good informant must possess the knowledge and experience required by the researcher; the informant should also be articulate, have the ability to reflect, be willing to participate in the study, and have the time to be interviewed. The study population was chosen from different grade levels in order to provide as much diversity as possible. Patton (1990) states that "there are no rules for sample size in qualitative inquiry. Sample size depends on what you want to know, the purpose of the inquiry, what's at stake, what will be useful, what will have credibility, and what can be done with available time and resources" (p. 184). This study group, while not a true "sample" representing the entire Arabic student population, presents a representative "snapshot" that will guide the reader vis-à-vis the population.

The acculturation theory for this qualitative study of Arab Americans is the single–continuum model of acculturation, and it is described as the changing of an ethnic traditional cultural trait for Anglo cultural traits. The exchange of cultural traits results in the individual becoming more Anglo in culture and is represented as a point on a continuum ranging from being unacculturated, bicultural, to acculturated, (Ponterotto, 2001).

    I used the CIPP (Contextual, Input, Process, and Product) model, an evaluation method used to appraise projects, developed by the Phi Delta National Study Committee on Evaluation, a group chaired by Daniel L. Stufflebeam. The CIPP model provided a conceptual framework, which I adapted for the qualitative paradigm. By utilizing the CIPP model to study the acculturation processes of Arabic children and their families in the United States School System, I obtained a thorough picture of the whole Arabic community

**Table 4**
Family Groups

| Families | City | State | Country of Origin | Number of Children Attending Public Schools |
|---|---|---|---|---|
| Family #1 | Pecan Valley Area | NM | Iraq | 5 |
| Family #2 | Pecan Valley Area | NM | Iraq | 4 |
| Family #3 | Pecan Valley Area | NM | Jordan | 2 |
| Family #4 | Pecan Valley Area | NM | Yemen | 3 |
| Family #5 | Pecan Valley Area | NM | Jordan | 3 |
| Family #6 | Pecan Valley Area | NM | Yemen | 4 |
| Family #7 | Pecan Valley Area | NM | Yemen | 4 |
| Family #8 | Pecan Valley Area | NM | Palestine | 4 |
| Family #9 | Pecan Valley Area | NM | Jordan | 1 |
| Family #10 | Pecan Valley Area | NM | Saudi Arabia | 3 |
| Family #11 | Pecan Valley Area | NM | Saudi Arabia | 1 |
| Family #12 | Pecan Valley Area | NM | Jordan | 2 |
| Family #13 | Pecan Valley Area | NM | Jordan | 2 |
| Family #14 | Pecan Valley Area | NM | Saudi Arabia | 1 |
| Family #15 | Pecan Valley Area | NM | Algeria | 4 |
| Family #16 | Hot City | TX | Iraq | 1 |
| Family #17 | Hot City | TX | Libya | 2 |
| Family #18 | Green City | NY | Palestine | 4 |
| Family #19 | Green City | NY | Palestine | 4 |
| Family #20 | Green City | NY | Sudan | 3 |
| Family #21 | Green City | NY | Jordan | 2 |
| Family #22 | Green City | NY | Sudan | 2 |
| Family #23 | Intermountain City | UT | Palestine | 2 |
| Family #24 | Intermountain City | UT | Egypt | 4 |
| Family #25 | Intermountain City | UT | Algeria | 1 |

## Participant Observation: Naturalistic Observation

The purpose of observational data is to gather information about the setting, the activities going on there, the individuals who are participating in the study, and the meaning of the observation. The role of the participant observer is either formal or informal (Gredler, 1996), and as the investigator of this study, I took part as a participant observer of the activities in the elementary school level classrooms. My observations took place at these levels because I wanted to see the acculturation processes of Arabic students during their early years; these were children who had come to the United States with little or no second language skills (English). As a participant observer, I personally viewed the social world of these students in their schools and family homes, and I spent time in educational settings like the Islamic Center of Pecan Valley.

In one public elementary school, I noted the application of the curriculum, observing the students and their teachers, a practice that Marshall and Rossman (1989) approve of, stating:

> Immersion in the setting allows the researcher to hear, see, and begin to experience reality as the participants do. Ideally, the researcher spends a considerable amount of time in the setting, learning about daily life. This technique for gathering data is basic to all qualitative research studies and forces a discussion of the role or stance of the researcher as a participant observer. (p. 79)

Worthen and Sanders (1987) express their concerns about merely observing, though, listing several other methods of qualitative research: running notes, a diary, notes on themes, schedules, and unobtrusive methods like asking questions, chatting, listening, etc. Jorgensen (1989) mentions that participant observers have direct experiences and observation methodologies, and participant observer methodology ranges from informal to formal interviews. As a participant observer, I had access to a wide collection of human communication documents, such as books, magazines, student handouts, syllabi, articles, etc. During my daily classroom observations that lasted for a month in the public schools, I had an opportunity to talk to Arabic students and ask them questions, thus acquiring real life interpretations about their schools, teachers, and curriculum. At the same time, I had the opportunity to talk to and interview the teachers in the public schools and in the Islamic Center in Pecan Valley.

**Documentation**

Bogdan and Biklen (1998) refer to documents as the materials that the qualitative researcher can use as a primary resource for collecting data. Indeed, collecting materials, records, and documents (official/unofficial documents of curriculum, regulations, directories, etc.) provide researchers with information that answer important questions throughout the study. Documentation also increases a researcher's knowledge and understanding of the curriculum. In this study, there was no significant official documentation referring to the Arabic students in schools; the only official documents that I obtained were those indicating the numbers of Arabic students in the public schools. Although, from the classroom, I obtained calendars, student homework, student logs, and class weekly agendas, and I had access to magazines and books when I observed at the Arabic school in Pecan Valley and the Intermountain public school.

**Interviewing**

Seidman (1998) defines interviewing as "a basic mode of inquiry. Recounting narratives of experience has been the major way throughout recorded history that humans made sense of their experience" (p. 2). Generally speaking, the purpose of interviewing is to know what the correspondents think, to know what their opinions and experiences are. Two interview types were used in this research study: standardized, open-ended ones and focus group discussions. For Patton (1990), standardized, open-ended interviews increase the probability of responses, reducing biases and facilitating organization and analyses of data in the process. Standardized, open-ended interviews were conducted on middle and high school Arabic students (Appendix C); I interviewed parents and their children regarding language preferences with this procedure as well (Appendix E). Open-ended interviews were also conducted on parents and their children (Appendix F) regarding their cultural preferences.

Seidman's three-interview series' procedures were used on the people in charge: principals, teachers, and tutors (Appendix B). Each interview lasted approximately 90 minutes, and the first interview focused on life history, the second covered experience, and the third dealt with reflection of meaning. By using Seidman's three-interview series, some interviews were done on the same day, while others were finished in three days (due to the time scheduling of teachers). I met some teachers on the same day of the interviews, but with others, I had to come back on the following day. So, the original procedure was modified to meet my time and also the teachers scheduling time. It wasn't exactly done the same way that Seidman proposed it, but it was modified according to my time and teachers free time. Also, sometimes the procedure didn't take the whole time (90 minutes), because the teachers were able to answer the three questions at the same time.

Through my observation at the Arabic school in the Pecan Valley Islamic Center, I had the chance to interview six teachers. The first three were mothers of students attending the public schools in the Pecan Valley area. The six teachers interviewed stated that the parents of Arabic students attending the public schools in the area were afraid that their children would lose their cultural and linguistic heritages; so, during the weekend, they sent their children to the Arabic school to learn about the Arabic language and culture. The parents also expressed the need for multicultural education at the public schools within designed curricula. The teacher interviews were recorded and then transcribed for data analysis (Table 1).

**Focus Group**

Krueger (1994) lists six characteristics of focus groups: (a) the people, (b) the assemblage into a series of groups, (c) the possession of certain characteristics, (d) the provision of data, (e) the qualitative nature, and (f) the focus in the discussion. A focus group, then, for Krueger is a carefully planned discussion designed to obtain perceptions on a defined area of interest in a permissive, non-threatening environment. It is conducted with approximately seven to ten people by a skilled interviewer. The discussion is comfortable, often enjoyable, for participants as they share their ideas and perceptions, and the group members influence each other by responding to each other's ideas and comments. Indeed, focus group interviews (Appendix D) strengthen the qualitative data through exploration, discovery, depth and interpretation (Morgan, 1998).

For my study using the CIPP model, focus group interviews (Table 2) were conducted on 15 fathers of kindergarten, elementary, middle or high school age students for three hours. The fathers were only from Jordan, Kuwait, Yemen, Iraq, Saudi Arabia, Egypt, Algeria, and Palestine. The interviewing took place in the Islamic Center of Pecan Valley. At this interview, I inquired about the fathers' opinions regarding the schools, its curriculum, their children, culture, and language, allowing for an open discussion; I designed open-ended interview questions for this matter, hoping to gather in-depth information through this group discussion, recording all interviews in the process. The interviewing was very interesting; it allowed me to ask many questions and get answers for the same questions from the fathers' different points of view. It was very interesting to listen to the fathers' concerns about the schools and their wishes that someday the Arabic heritage would be included within the school's curriculum. It was very interesting to have me, as a mother, teacher and a female, among 15 fathers and hear different gender points of view concerning the male and female children.

The discussion within the focus group was very interesting, especially when the fathers talked about schools, teachers, teacher/parent conferences, and the barriers at school regarding their children's education. They all insisted on their loyalty to the Arabic language and culture. Also, it was intriguing to see how they wanted their children to learn about their heritage's background and ways to teach their children about them.

**Data Analysis (from the CIPP model)**

Data analysis involves content analysis, a search for larger patterns where meaning resides, and the researcher must read and re-read the transcripts of the interviews from the families (Appendices E & F), students (Appendix C) and teachers (Appendix B). The researcher also has to examine observations (Table 1) and notes of documentation in consequence. For Bogdan and Biklen (1998), data analysis is:

> The process of systematically searching and arranging the interview transcripts, fieldstones, and other material that you accumulate to increase your own understanding of them and enable you to present what you have discovered to others. Analysis involves working with the data, organizing them, breaking into manageable units, synthesizing them, searching of patterns, discovering what is important and what is learned and deciding what you will tell others. (p. 157)

Qualitative data analysis has some form of inductive analysis. Indeed, the researcher attempts to understand the delineating curriculum context, inputs, processes, and products through data analysis from transcribed interviews and field notes from the observation of all sample groups (parents, students, and eight teachers). Qualitative data analysis is conducted during or after the study, intent on answering the study's questions; it involves organizing and reducing the information for the purpose of interpretation, drawing conclusions from various qualitative methods used throughout the study (Bogdan & Biklen, 1998).

**Triangulation of Summative Research**

Triangulation "is a process by which a researcher can guard against accusation that a study's findings are simply an artifact of a single method, a single source, or a single investigator biases" (Patton, 1990, p. 470); thus, it is important that researchers rely on more than one source of information for the study. Triangulation is obtained by comparing the different data resources used in the qualitative study, and comparative analysis of the different data collection methods significantly increases the overall credibility of the study. "Validity and reliability" in this evaluative study depends on the methodological skills and integrity of the researcher (Uwe, 1998), and skillful interviewing, observations, and documentation analyses, in conjunction with responsible data analysis and triangulation, ensures that the study will be valid and reliable. I obtained triangulation from the summative research that was amassed during the qualitative study: field notes from the home and classroom observations in Pecan Valley and Intermountain City; audio recordings from the interviews in the Pecan Valley Islamic Center, Pecan Valley and Intermountain City public school systems, and family interviews in Hot City, Green City, and Intermountain City; and transcriptions from these interviews.

**Confidentiality and Protection of
Subjects Privacy**

The Institutional Review Board approved my research to use human subjects in research (Appendix G). The subjects of the study were parents, their children, principals, teachers, and tutors. The participation in this qualitative study was voluntary, and each individual was protected by fictitious names and settings. No money was involved. Each subject's personal privacy was also protected, and they signed consent forms (Appendices H-K) before participating in the study; a description of the findings is available to them upon completion of this research.

**Summary**

The CIPP research approach, based on the axiom, to improve, not prove, has helped schools, institutions, and agencies conduct a wide range of evaluations, and I have used this model qualitatively to study the acculturation processes of Arabic students in language and culture, discovering curriculum weaknesses and strengths in the process. Through the CIPP model of research, I found that the Arabic students and their parents were aware of how their culture was being assimilated into mainstream American society within the public schools. The students and their parents felt that this was due, in part, to the teachers' lack of knowledge concerning the linguistic and cultural heritages of the Arabic people. Consequently, most Arabic students experienced a sense of cultural shock due to the stereotypical curricula of the public schools. Also, many of the teachers interviewed admitted that they lacked knowledge about the Arabic culture.

## CHAPTER 4
## FINDINGS

This qualitative study of the Arabic language and culture took place in four states: New Mexico, Texas, Utah, and New York. The acculturation theory for this qualitative study of Arab American is the single–continuum model of acculturation, and it is described as the changing of an ethnic traditional cultural trait to an Anglo cultural trait. The exchange of cultural traits results in the individual becoming more like the Anglo culture, and it is represented as a point on a continuum ranging from being unacculturated, bicultural, to acculturated (Ponterotto, 2001).

For this qualitative study on the acculturation of Arabic students and their families in the United States, based upon my assumptions of the process of acculturation of Arab Americans, I was guided by the following questions used to research the Arabic students, their parents, and the teachers in the public school systems.

1. How much acculturation from a culture and a language point of view do Arabic students face in the public schools and nationwide?
2. What are some of the challenges Arabic students encounter in their schooling processes in the United States?
3. Do these difficulties change the parents', students', and teachers' learning environments?

4. Does ignoring the Arabic language and culture influence the parents and their children in the public schools?

In answering these questions, the CIPP model was used as a tool to study the target population. The four phases (Contextual, Input, Process, and Product) of the model enriched my study by supplying a huge amount of information about the target samples. The four stages of the original model are: Contextual, Input, Process, and Product (Madaus, 1983). I used the original CIPP model with some modification to meet the needs of my research investigation on the acculturation of Arabic families and their children in language and culture within the United States.

The information obtained through my qualitative research on the acculturation of Arabic students and their families was from triangulation, a summative research tool focusing on students, parents, teachers, and focus groups (Table 5). In Pecan Valley, New Mexico, I interviewed family members in their homes using open-ended questions (Appendices E & F) and observed how both the assimilation and acculturation of Arabic students in the public school system affected their language and cultural values. I also noted after interviewing Pecan Valley public school teachers (Appendix B) that curriculum assimilation often led to a lack of knowledge about the culture of Arabic students. At the Islamic Center in Pecan Valley, I interviewed teachers (Appendix B) and noted their belief that there was a stronger need for multicultural education in the public schools. I also interviewed the focus group (Table 2) at the Pecan Valley Islamic Center, using open-ended questions (Appendix D), and covered issues like public school curriculum assimilation, stereotyping, and cultural shock. My interviewing of Pecan Valley students with open-ended questions (Appendix C) covered the same issues as the focus group.

In Hot City, Texas, Green City, New York, and Intermountain City, Utah, I interviewed families using open-ended questions (Appendices E & F) and asked them about topics ranging from language assimilation to the acculturation of the Arabic language and culture in the public school system. In Intermountain City, we also covered issues like cultural shock and stereotyping. Also, I observed classroom proceedings and interviewed teachers (Appendix B) at the Intermountain public schools and discovered that curriculum assimilation led to a lack of knowledge about the Arabic culture.

Overall, my findings revealed that Arabic student identities, products of both language and culture, are often not incorporated into the public school classrooms; more importantly, they are absent from either bilingual or multicultural education. This lack of identity within the schools causes feelings of distress and insecurity within Arabic students, regardless of age. When the school curriculum excludes Arabic students, it, in a sense, perpetuates the stereotyping that they experience from their peers, teachers, and society. Feagin and Booher (2003) explain that tensions may erupt between Arab Americans and educators when "teachers are unaware that their Arab students come from numerous countries and cultures or when teachers make incorrect assumptions about the cultural backgrounds of their students" (p. 334). Indeed, the lack of an Arabic voice in the classroom may engender feelings of resentment among Arabic students and their parents.

I found that among parents, they wanted their children to be aware of the Arabic language and culture. Cultural awareness and language loyalty were obvious when dealing with the Arabic families in all four states. Language and cultural loyalty arose when the parent expressed fear that their children were losing their Arabic heritage of language and culture. Interaction with other ethnicities was something the parents and their children always preferred. They liked to use English but at the same time, wanted to read, write, and speak Arabic. Like any other person living in the United States, they all felt stress from their environment, work/school, family, health, and financial issues in their daily lives. In addition, their acculturation process got more stressful with acculturative stress from their immigration status, culture shock, and minority status (Padilla, 1986, p.101-120).

In Banks' (1988) model of multicultural education, he feels that the schools must recognize Arabic heroes and holidays, something that they currently fail to do. Indeed, Arabic heroes and holidays are completely unrecognized in the public school bilingual or multicultural classroom, an oversight justified by the statement that religion has no place in education, a supposition weakened by the fact that Christmas, Easter, and Hanukkah are observed by the school systems.

## Curriculum and Assimilation: CIPP
## Research of Language and Culture

In my study on public school curriculum, I followed the CIPP model of evaluation, using it as a tool to research the assimilation processes of Arabic students in the public schools. In the first stage, contextual research, I studied the target population, noting their linguistic and cultural needs and problems with the school curriculum. Generally, the public schools did not possess significant documentation on Arabic children, and the only kind that I did find dealt with the number of students from Arabic countries.

I utilized the second part of the CIPP model, Input, by observing elementary school children, noting that a great deal of the curriculum input was not relevant to the Arabic students, either linguistically or culturally. Many academic classes, including reading, writing, science, math, spelling, and music, did not address the Arabic students' backgrounds. Indeed, the curriculum input was designed to foster the Americanization and assimilation of these students into the dominant society, realizing that this input encouraged the Arabic students to master the English language. Based on my interviews with the teachers, I learned that only a few tried to understand their Arabic students' language and culture, but that, of course, was not significant enough to learn about their students; most teachers were not even aware of the Arabic language and culture.

The third level of the CIPP model of research is process, an outline of procedures for curriculum implementation, a way in which Arabic students can learn through various methods of curriculum implementation. A few of these methods include: technological innovations, computer use, and video programming. Teacher or student presentations, peer groups, cooperative sessions, and field trips are additional methods of learning, and my classroom observations revealed that the curriculum implementation procedures were used to teach students the language and culture of the dominant societal group.

The last phase of the study, product evaluation consists of the previous phases; it is a summative evaluation of the Arabic students from different aspects. While studying the Arabic students and their processes of acculturation, I came to realize that the public school curriculum forced the Arabic students to assimilate into the dominant culture because there were no other choices. During the interviews, the parents insisted that the schools were ignorant of their cultural identities, mainly because their language and culture were not addressed at all. Thus, the children became more fluent in English than their own language, assimilating into the dominant culture, ignoring their cultural heritages in the process. Indeed, the curriculum itself was designed to encourage student assimilation into the dominant society, whether Native American, African American, Caucasian, Asian, or Arabic, and most of the teachers implemented the curriculum without considering alternative methodologies to introduce students into the Arabic culture.

Table 5
*Findings (Summative Research)*

| CIPP Model of Research of Language and Culture | Settings | Qualitative Measurements | Type of Qualitative Measurement | Findings (Summative Research) |
|---|---|---|---|---|
| Contextual & Input Research at home of Language and Culture | Family Homes in Pecan Valley | Participant Observation | Home Observation of Language & culture | 1-Assimilation of Language 2-Acculturation (language and culture |
| Contextual, Input, Process, and Product research | Arabic School in Islamic Center in Pecan Valley, Weekend Basis | Participant Observation, Interviews & Documentations | Classroom Observation & Teachers Interviews, Seidman procedure | 1-Public school curriculum Assimilation 2-The need for Multicultural education |
| Contextual, Input, Process, and Product research | Pecan Valley Public Schools | Teachers Interviews Documentation | Teacher Interviews with Seidman Procedure | 1-Curriculum assimilation 2-Lack of knowledge of Arabic and Arabic culture |
| Contextual, Input, & Product at Home of language and Culture | Family Homes in Pecan Valley Area | Interviews & Participant Observation | With Open-Ended Questions | 1-Assimilation of language 2-Acculturation of language and culture |
| Contextual, Input, & Product research at home of language and Culture | Children Interviews in Pecan Valley Area | Interviews & Participant Observation | With Open-Ended Questions | 1-Language and culture assimilation at school 2- Acculturation of language and culture at home 3-Stereotyping 4-Cultural shock 5-Teachers lack of knowledge of Arabic and Arabic culture |
| Contextual &Input, Process and product of language and Culture. | Focus Group in Islamic Center in Pecan Valley Area | Interviews Observation & Interviews | Open-Ended Questions | 1-Public school curriculum assimilation 2-School is a good place to learn 3- Stereotyping 4-Cultural shock 5-Teachers lack of knowledge of Arabic and Arabic culture |

Table 5 (continued)

| CIPP Model of Research of Language and Culture | Settings | Qualitative Measurements | Type of Qualitative Measurement | Findings (Summative Research) |
|---|---|---|---|---|
| Contextual &Input, Process and product of language and Culture | Arabic School in Islamic Center in Pecan Valley area; weekends only | Interviews | Participant Observer Seidmen Procedure | 1-Public school curriculum assimilation 2-The need for multicultural education |
| Contextual & input research of Language and Culture | Families Interviews in Hot City/TX | Interviews | Open-Ended Questions | 1-Language assimilation 2-Acculturation of language and culture 3-School is a good place to learn |
| Contextual & Input and product of Language and Culture at Home | Families Interviews in Green City | Teacher Interviews & Classroom observation | Open-Ended Questions | 1-Assimilation of Language 2-Acculturation (language and culture |
| Contextual & Input, process and Product of Language and Culture | Intermountain Public School | Interviews | Seidman Procedure Participant observer | 1-Lack of knowledge of Arabic and Arabic culture 2-Curriculum assimilation |
| Contextual &Input and Product of Language at home | Families Interviews in Intermountain City | Interviews | Open-Ended Questions | 1-Assimilation of Language 2-Acculturation (language and culture 3-School is a good place to learn 4-Cultural shock 5-Stereotyping |

### Interviews with Students of Middle
### and High Schools: CIPP Research

Through my interviews, I learned that a number of the surveyed Arabic students were new arrivals into the United States, individuals whose parents were seeking their PhDs; the other Arabic students had been in the country for an extended period of time, children of parents who were working as business associates, medical personnel, university teachers, computer specialists, etc. These families were citizens, non-citizens, and resident aliens of the United States, and they originated from different Arabic Middle Eastern countries, places where a single language and culture created the domain of their society, language, and culture.

The Arabic children attended different school levels, ranging from kindergarten to high school, places where their identities were often unrecognized. Indeed, most of my interviews with the teachers indicated that they did not know anything about the culture or language of their Arabic students, mainly because the schools rarely recognized them. Despite this, the Arabic children, starting from the earliest grades, did try hard to understand the new languages, whether English or Spanish; a major motivator stemmed from the fact that English was the dominant language.

After interviewing Arabic middle and high school students, I learned that they all agreed that public schooling was a great place to learn, appreciating its provision of opportunities to prepare for future career choices; they also discussed the positive and negative sides of public education, and from their points of view, they liked the flexibility of choosing their own electives, consequently selecting those courses that would benefit them in the long run. As a result of the elective selections, the students also felt that they could choose classes at their own capability levels. The students also expressed an interest in activities geared toward helping them understand the curriculum, and the availability of different school clubs let them explore subjects of personal interest.

The students interviewed also expressed a respect for their school teachers, noting their instructors' attempts to clarify the material for them, thus ensuring that the Arabic students could master their assigned subjects. Indeed, since many of the students were from different cultures, a few of the teachers tried to integrate their Arabic students, learning their holidays, culture, and language, and the students expressed their gratitude, revealing that many instructors helped them make up what they missed.

Some Arabic students once attended schools in the Middle East, institutions where they had to wear school uniforms. From the interviews, I learned that many of the students approved of the fact that a number of educational institutions in the United Stated had started enforcing dress codes as well; the Arabic students in the Middle East had had official uniforms in their school systems since kindergarten, and consequently, the idea of dress codes were familiar to the Arabic students living in the United States.

The students also described the negative aspects of schooling because many of them had experienced culture shock while attending the U.S. public school systems. For instance, the male and female students were often separated until the university level in the Middle East, and if there was coeducation there, it was because of poverty in rural areas. Indeed, there was no money to provide a different school for each gender. Although, coeducation was also found in American- and European-style schools within the Middle Eastern countries, places where children whose parents worked in the Middle East were attending school.

Most Arabic students experienced culture shock while in the U.S. public school systems, especially those children whose parents had moved to the United States after they had attended the Arabic schools. Most patterns of cultural shock dealt with male/female relationships. Indeed, one female high school student said:

" I don't like that much about school. I was in culture shock when I came here from school in Libya. Here in school you, see 11th and 12th graders hugging, kissing, smoking; also, you can see pregnant teens in schools."

Another pattern of culture shock centered on the violence and gangs within the schools. Some students said that this phenomenon made them scared because they had never experienced that before; they grew up in schools that were very safe, places where all of the students learned the same Arabic language, living under one cultural norm in the process.

Another cultural shock experienced by the students occurred after their exposure to the apparently lenient rules within the U.S. public schools; their home schools in the Middle East were more restrictive and disciplined in nature. One high school student commented:

"Rules are not effective. When any student does something wrong it is because it is easy to do."

The students also considered the attention paid to sporting activities excessive and shocking. In their home countries, academics were their main focus, not sports. One high school student said:

"Schools give more attention to sport's activities than academic achievement. They give scholarships based on who is good at sports."

A few of the interviewed students felt targeted by stereotyping as well, stating that some of their teachers expressed derogatory ideas about Arabs and Middle Eastern people. One female high school student proclaimed:

"Some teachers are understanding while others are racist. At times, when they talk about political issues concerning the Middle East, I have to face the teacher talking about it, looking at me and saying to the whole class that Arabs are really bad, even when they know that I am Arabic."

Also, a number of the Arabic students observed that the school history books mainly talked about United States history, ignoring histories from different cultures and countries in the process, information that the students wanted to learn more about. Indeed, the students felt that a lack of knowledge about other countries caused harm, mainly because it made it easier to lie about other cultures. Also, the curriculum of social science classes did not allow teachers to introduce other languages and cultures, a fact upheld in spite of the fact that the public schools were of mixed ethnicity (Table 6)

**Table 6**
*Study Group of Middle and High School Students*

| The Middle and High School Students | City | State | Country of Origin | Gender |
|---|---|---|---|---|
| Student #1 | Pecan Valley Area | NM | Iraq | M |
| Student #2 | Pecan Valley Area | NM | Iraq | M |
| Student #3 | Pecan Valley Area | NM | Iraq | M |
| Student #4 | Pecan Valley Area | NM | Iraq | M |
| Student #5 | Pecan Valley Area | NM | Iraq | M |
| Student #6 | Pecan Valley Area | NM | Iraq | F |
| Student #7 | Pecan Valley Area | NM | Iraq | F |
| Student #8 | Pecan Valley Area | NM | Iraq | F |
| Student #9 | Pecan Valley Area | NM | Iraq | M |
| Student #10 | Pecan Valley Area | NM | Yemen | M |
| Student #11 | Pecan Valley Area | NM | Yemen | M |
| Student #12 | Pecan Valley Area | NM | Yemen | M |
| Student #14 | Pecan Valley Area | NM | Yemen | M |
| Student #15 | Pecan Valley Area | NM | Yemen | M |
| Student #16 | Pecan Valley Area | NM | Yemen | M |
| Student #17 | Pecan Valley Area | NM | Yemen | M |
| Student #18 | Pecan Valley Area | NM | Palestine | F |
| Student #19 | Pecan Valley Area | NM | Palestine | F |
| Student #20 | Pecan Valley Area | NM | Algeria | F |
| Student #21 | Pecan Valley Area | NM | Algeria | M |
| Student #23 | Pecan Valley | NM | Algeria | M |
| Student #22 | Pecan Valley Area | NM | Algeria | M |
| Student #24 | Hot City | TX | Libya | M |
| Student #25 | Green City | NY | Palestine | M |
| Student #26 | Green City | NY | Palestine | M |
| Student #27 | Green City | NY | Palestine | M |
| Student #28 | Green City | NY | Palestine | M |
| Student #29 | Green City | NY | Palestine | M |
| Student #30 | Green City | NY | Palestine | M |
| Student #31 | Green City | NY | Palestine | M |
| Student #32 | Green City | NY | Palestine | M |
| Student #33 | Green City | NY | Sudan | M |
| Student #34 | Green City | NY | Sudan | M |
| Student #35 | Green City | NY | Sudan | M |
| Student #36 | Green City | NY | Jordan | M |
| Student #37 | Green City | NY | Jordan | M |
| Student #38 | Green City | NY | Sudan | M |
| Student #39 | Green City | NY | Sudan | M |
| Student #40 | Intermountain City | UT | Egypt | F |
| Student #41 | Intermountain City | UT | Egypt | F |
| Student #42 | Intermountain City | UT | Egypt | F |
| Student #43 | Intermountain City | UT | Egypt | M |
| Student #44 | Intermountain City | UT | Egypt | F |

**Interviews with Teachers: CIPP Research**

The teacher interviews were very interesting, enabling me to understand their ideas and opinions concerning Arabic students in the kindergarten, elementary, middle, and high school levels. I selected the group of public school teachers by visiting them in their school settings (Table 7). In Pecan Valley and Intermountain City, I knew the teachers personally, and the teachers surveyed ran classes that were English only, bilingual (English/Spanish), or dual language (English/Spanish), but I only interviewed teachers who had had experience with Arabic students in their classes.

The children at the Pecan Valley Islamic Center only attended during the weekends, and the teachers at the Arabic school taught their students about the Arabic culture and language. The parents sent their children to there because they feared that their children were losing their language and culture. Indeed, the parents felt that the public schools did not address these issues in their curriculum

At the kindergarten level, the teachers did inform me that they had taught students from all over the Middle East, especially from the Arabic countries, and these students arrived with very little English, if any. Some of them had been in the United States for barely two or three days, creating problems because the teachers had little or no knowledge of the Arabic language or culture. One dual language Kindergarten teacher said:

> This is my third year of teaching Arabic children. I don't know a lot about Arabic children. I wish I knew more; as a matter of fact, I took a multicultural class in the summer, and in the multicultural class, they said that there are no steps to take to learn these things: culture and language. This is just as

important for children coming from Mexico. There aren't any teachers that know the Arabic language or culture here, so we concentrate on English and Spanish instead.

The teachers also admitted that the Arabic students, after arriving into the country, were exposed to only the English language or the English/Spanish programs. They did note that the Arabic students adapted very well to English, though.

At the elementary level, the Arabic students also adjusted to the school culture very well. Indeed, the Arabic students shared in all of the holiday celebrations.

One second-grade teacher explained:

"I have one Arabic child. The children at school participate in the celebrations of the USA. I wish that their parents would come and share their celebration with us. I would like to learn more about the Arabic language and culture."

Teacher awareness about the Arabic culture was rare, thus ensuring that the school curriculum dealt only with English or Spanish. In consequence, the elementary level Arabic students had to adapt to the dominant language and culture, something that a second grade teacher illustrated by describing one female Arabic student:

"Me and most of the children in the class don't know about her culture. She is excited to tell us and we are very interested; she talked about Ramadan. She doesn't have really an accent when speaking, so they don't know that she is from a different culture because she is just like them."

In the interviews, many teachers noted that the white students were the majority of the schools' populations, something that they commented would change, though, as different cultures continued to emigrate into the United States. In one interview with a second grade teacher, she said:

"Schools have become more and more populated with children of different nationalities. Before, we just had white children. We have been isolated because we dealt mainly with white children. Now, we have Hispanic, Arabic, African American, Asian, and Native American."

Another second grade teacher revealed:

"My school has few non-white, non-Christian students. In the second grade level, we teach about communities, rural and city (urban) life. Although, we don't have many multicultural experiences in our rural school."

At the middle and high school levels, there were few programs centering on other cultures. The main Bilingual/ESL programs focused on English and Spanish, consequently making teachers the primary source for multicultural education. One bilingual teacher said:

> My experience with different children was positive. At the beginning, I learned a lot about the children's cultures in reading books to know about religion and food. I did it on my own individual level. I need to know more about the children's cultures, especially in reading books and stories. I brought pictures to the class, like camels, and the students used to laugh.

The newcomers from Arabic countries were faced with large school and class sizes, especially in the middle and high school levels, thus bringing the language issue quickly into the forefront. However, their adjustment to the language was fast, quicker if they had had some English in their backgrounds. Cultural differences, on the other hand, remained issues for a longer period of time; in most cases, they stood as barriers for students trying to accept the American culture, mainly because their was a lack of multicultural education in the schools. Indeed, in many educational facilities, neither the culture nor the language of the international students were addressed, causing one high school student to proclaim that

> I don't know if the students have problems with the language. They speak English very well and are well educated. Here in the schools, the majority culture is the dominant culture. If a girl comes from an Arabic country, wearing a scarf or covering her whole body, the kids make fun; some will ask about it, while a few will respect her, but it is from outside of the majority and school culture.

**Table 7:** Teachers group

| Teachers, Tutors & Principals | Level of Teaching | Gender | City | State |
|---|---|---|---|---|
| Teacher #1 | High School | F | Pecan Valley Area | NM |
| Tutor #1 | Elementary | F | Pecan Valley Area | NM |
| Tutor #2 | Elementary | F | Pecan Valley Area | NM |
| Tutor #3 | Elementary | F | Pecan Valley Area | NM |
| Tutor #4 | Elementary | F | Pecan Valley Area | NM |
| Teacher #2 | Elementary (Kinder-Garden) | F | Pecan Valley Area | NM |
| Teacher #3 | Elementary (1st Grade) | F | Pecan Valley Area | NM |
| Teacher #4 | Middle School (8$^{th}$ Grade Science Teacher) | M | Pecan Valley Area | NM |
| Teacher #5 | Elementary (dual Language Kinder-Garden) | F | Pecan Valley Area | NM |
| Teacher #6 | Middle School (BIL. ESL) | F | Pecan Valley Area | NM |
| Teacher #7 | Elementary (2nd Dual Language) | F | Pecan Valley Area | NM |
| Teacher #8 | Elementary (2nd Language BIL) | F | Islamic Center in Pecan Valley Area | NM |
| Teacher #9 | Elementary (1$^{st}$ & 2$^{nd}$) | F | Islamic Center in Pecan Valley Area | NM |
| Teacher #10 | Elementary (1$^{st}$ & 2$^{nd}$) | F | Islamic Center in Pecan Valley Area | NM |
| Teacher #11 | Elementary (1$^{st}$ & 2$^{nd}$) | F | Islamic Center in Pecan Valley Area | NM |
| Teacher #12 | Elementary (1$^{st}$ & 2$^{nd}$) | F | Islamic Center in Pecan Valley Area | NM |
| Teacher #13 | Elementary (1$^{st}$ & 2$^{nd}$) | F | Islamic Center in Pecan Valley Area | NM |
| Principal #1 | High School | M | Pecan Valley Area | NM |
| Principal #2 | High School | M | Pecan Valley Area | NM |
| Principal #3 | Elementary | F | Intermountain City | UT |
| Teacher #14 | Elementary (2$^{nd}$ Grade) | F | Intermountain City | UT |

**Focus Group Interviews: CIPP Research**

Through focus group interviews with fifteen fathers in the Pecan Valley Islamic Center (Table 2), I realized that they had three different concerns: curriculum implementation, the teachers, and their involvement with the schools regarding the future educations of their children.

The fathers, for the most part, were pleased that their children were learning English in the schools, mainly because it enriched their learning processes, but I did find that some fathers from Yemen and Kuwait and Saudi Arabia did not want their children assimilated into the public schools. Instead, they preferred home schooling because it let them teach their children the Arabic language and culture.

At the high school levels, most of the fathers said that the system was very good. They liked that in the last two years of high school, the students were allowed to enroll in courses connected to the university, good experiences for their future specializations. Although, some fathers voiced their concerns that there were no assigned textbooks in the curriculum for their children, especially in the elementary school levels, preventing fathers from following up on their children's exercises. Indeed, they were dissatisfied with the assigned handouts because their children could lose them.

The fathers also felt that the school assessment processes of their children were not clear, consequently preventing them from knowing if their children were ready to move from one grade level to another. The numbers that were provided in the class progress reports did not give them any indication of teacher satisfaction concerning their children's progress in school. Thus, the fathers of Arabic children felt that there should be another way to evaluate the students at school.

Also, they were concerned about the school curriculum, one that ignored their culture and language. For example, the fathers noted that in the ESL programs, the children were treated as if Spanish, not Arabic, was their first language. Indeed, one father stated:

> At school, in ESL classes, my children were learning Spanish. At the first moment, my children got confused because they don't know English or Spanish; so, the children ended knowing nothing. For that reason, I think, the schools should have ESL integration with Arabic for our Arabic children; otherwise, our children will be lost.

The fathers did say that some of the teachers were open and helpful, caring about their children's individual needs. But others, they noted, treated them like foreigners, indicating that they did not know anything about the schools. For example, one father, whose son was in middle school, had a problem centering on the fact that his child did not want to attend dance classes. Because of a cultural point of view, his son could not dance with any girl who was not a close relative. The father stated:

> My son was crying when he came back home from school because he didn't want to dance. I went to the teachers and told them that my son didn't want to dance. The teachers told me that this course was a requirement and that the people living in the area paid money for it for their children. It took me a hard time to convince them not to force my son to dance. I think that they should understand some cultural sensitivity aspects for children.

Another father concluded:

They have to be honest when treating foreign kids; my kids came to me and said that the teacher forced them to eat pork. I told the teachers before that we don't eat pork or ham, but the teacher treated them the opposite way. One of my children told me that his teacher told him to eat the meat and not to throw it away.

Another concern that the fathers had expressed dealt with sex education, a topic that was culturally unacceptable to discuss in public; the parents did not want their children exposed to sex education because in Arabic cultures, sex was restricted to marriage. Consequently, the fathers felt that exposing their children to sex education at an early age would be both a distraction and ethically unacceptable. One parent said:

"Sex education is not education. It is bigger than education. It is worse than education. It is teaching the children to do what they shouldn't do."

In addition to the concerns voiced by the fathers, they also offered many suggestions about what they could do as a group, emphasizing the need for strong involvement within the schools. One father commented:

In the elementary level, there should be a kind of involvement, but more involvement is needed at middle and high school levels. My children and I together could decide suitable courses for his/her future. Also, I should see which clubs my children could attend before and after school time. If I do not get involved with my children in school, I know they would be lost.

At the same time, fathers had strong feelings about working together as a group; they suggested going to speak at the schools, bringing awareness to the administrators, principals, and teachers about the Arabic culture in consequence.

**Language Preference: CIPP Research**

I studied language preferences from the parent and child perspectives, using two methods; first, I spent time with Arabic families in their homes, observing the on-going communications (the spoken language) inside the family unit; second, I conducted open-ended questions (Appendix E). My observations (Table 4) inside the family homes revealed that the communications between the mother and the father took place in Arabic. When the mother or the father left home for work, though, they used English as their communicating language. Indeed, they also reverted to English in outside environments like the neighbors' houses, shopping centers, restaurants, etc. For the most part, the father always knew English; sometimes, the mother did not, limiting their communication to the home, speaking only to those who understand Arabic.

On the other hand, for families who had lived in the country for a longer period of time, the situation was very different; the mother's communication with outside home environments was much better, mainly because she understood and spoke English more fluently. Indeed, for parents, especially the mothers, the duration of time spent in the United States made a huge difference in respect to their outside communications. Although, the language of the fathers was always better because they usually came to the United States as students, seeking educational or business opportunities. Furthermore, in many cases, both parents were either going to school or working professionally. They spoke English because they were students, school professors, doctors, etc.

In my interviews with both parents, most preferred to speak their first language; they considered it the main language at home, speaking it most of the time. Arabic was also the main language for reading, writing, and subscribing. Also, they opted to listen to music or the news on the Arabic channels available through the Satellite systems. In addition, Arabic was the language of communication between Arabic families. Although, it was different with friends of other languages; then, the language mainly occurred in English.

Arabic children, on the other hand, preferred to speak in English. The children, from preschool to high school, chose to communicate with their parents, siblings, and friends in English. My observations with the open-ended interviews revealed that the Arabic children, depending on where they spent their childhoods, could be classified into three groups according to language preferences:

1. Arabic children who were born and raised in the United States.
2. Arabic children who were partially raised outside of the United States (mainly in their native countries).
3. Arabic adults who where born in the country but spent their childhood in their parents' native Arabic countries.

The first category, Arabic children born and raised in the United States, were from different grades, ranging from pre-school to high school. These children consequently went to public school since their earliest years, exposed to the official language of the public school systems, English, in consequence. They spent a good deal of their time at school or with their friends, using English most of the time, and the social life surrounding this group of children had a great influence on their preference for English. In my observation within the home settings, the children communicated in English among themselves, and when the parents communicated with them in Arabic, they responded back in English.

The children that I interviewed from the first group were mainly middle or high school students. In the interviews, they indicated that they opted to speak in English; some did not even know Arabic. Unlike their parents, they preferred to listen to television channels in English

The second group, the Arabic children who came with their parents to the United States, emigrated here because at least one of their parents was seeking an educational degree or occupational opportunity. This group of children spent part of their education in their native countries, continuing their schooling upon arrival into the United States, and they ranged from elementary to high school ages.

The duration of time each child from the second group stayed in the United States had its influence on her/his language preference, allowing the student to speedily pick up English. In my observation, the language preference of these students was similar to the first group, and the school and social interactions occurring there helped them acclimate themselves to English, using it at home in consequence.

As mentioned with the first group, the second set preferred to use English at school or with their friends, opting to read, write, and listen to the Satellite TV in English as well. These children, who came to the USA during their middle or high school years, still had the capacity to speak in Arabic, but never forgot to utilize English, the dominant language.

The third group, those children born in the United States but raised in the Middle Eastern Arabic countries, spent most of their childhood abroad. They returned to the United States with their parents, individuals who were seeking to study or to work in the country. The children's ages ranged from eight to 18 years old, and after being in the country, learning English from the school or their peer social groups, they still corresponded with their parents in Arabic. My open-ended interviews revealed that this group of children and adults used both English and Arabic in their daily communications, and while at home, they listened to both the Arabic and English TV and Satellite Channels.

They used English at school and Arabic at home. They spoke Arabic with those who knew the language, reverting to English with non-Arabic speakers. The third group of children and adults also preferred to use both languages when subscribing, reading, writing, and listening to the radio, conversations, or television. Subsequently, both languages, English and Arabic, were preferable for them.

**Cultural Preference: CIPP Research**

This qualitative study of the Arabic language and culture took place in four states: New Mexico, Texas, Utah, and New York. The acculturation theory for this qualitative study of Arab Americans is the single–continuum model of acculturation, and it is described as the changing of an ethnic cultural trait for an Anglo cultural trait. The exchange of cultural traits causes an individual to become more like the Anglo culture, and it is represented as a point on a continuum ranging from being unacculturated, bicultural, to acculturated (Ponterotto, 2001).

For this qualitative study on the acculturation of Arabic students and their families in the United States, based upon my assumptions of the process of acculturation of Arab Americans, the following questions were used to research the Arabic students, their parents, and the teachers in the public school systems.

1. How much acculturation from a culture and a language point of view do Arabic students face in the public schools and nationwide?
2. What are some of the challenges Arabic students encounter in their schooling processes in the United States?
3. Do these difficulties change the parents', students', and teachers' learning environments?
4. Does ignoring the Arabic language and culture influence the parents and their children in the public schools?

In studying the parents' cultural preferences for their children, I developed a series of open-ended interview questions (Appendix F) for the parents and their children, selecting eight norms outlined by Dana (2000), studying the cultural preferences of these two groups as a result. The norms that I used to study the cultural preference were the following:

1. Ethnic group: what the interviewee considers herself/himself to belong to.
2. What ethnic group does the interviewee choose to be close friends with?

3. What other ethnic groups do the interviewee choose to befriend?
4. Faith Practice preferences? If the interviewee is still performing prayers, attending the mosque.
5. Food preferences? If the interviewee eats only Arabic food, mixed ethnicities food, eat Holy forbidden food like Pork or drink Alcohol.
6. Scarf-wearing preference for females? If the Arabic female likes to or not cover her head.
7. Music preferences? What music he/she likes to listen to.
8. Marriage preferences? If the interviewee like of his /her spouse to be from Arabic or other ethnicities

My analysis centered on the parents and the grown childrens' responses to the questions; I placed the parents in one group and their mature children in another in order to see the acculturation between both groups.

### Cultural Preference of Parents

The parents' group tended to possess similar cultural preference in three of the eight norms. Both parents viewed her/himself as an Arab or Arab American, depending on whether she/he was a citizen of the United States or not. Also, it was clear that they preferred marriages within the same ethnic and religious groups, selecting individuals practicing their faith in the Islamic centers. I also found that parents from Saudi Arabia, Yemen, and Kuwait felt more like their identities were being lost because of the acculturating influences within the United States.

In addition, the majority of women that I interviewed (25 total) opted to wear scarves; only three out of the 25 women did not prefer it, and they did not wear the scarf because they did not feel comfortable wearing it among the dominant society. There were exceptions for every cultural norm, but I chose the responses of the sample majority to determine the preferences of this group.

The parents' multi-dimensional cultural norm preferences for food did not include pork or alcohol, and they had friends from both Arabic and non-Arabic groups. Also, the parents enjoyed listening to music from different cultures.

**Cultural Preference of Adult Children**

The age of the grown children in the Arabic families ranged from 12 to 18. I interviewed each of the families' sons and daughters, totaling 44 students from the middle or high schools in the process. Among the 44 students, ten were female students. In analyzing the data that I had acquired from the designed open-ended interviews, I divided the Arabic adult children into two groups according to their cultural norm preferences. Just like their parents, the Arabic mature children noted that they belonged to the Arab or Arab American ethnicities. Moreover, they shared the same beliefs as their parents concerning the faith practices in the Islamic centers, believing that marriage should be from the same Arabic ethnicities.

In wearing the scarves, the majority of female daughters from this age group differed from their mothers, choosing not to wear it in their daily lives because they did not feel comfortable wearing it out in public.

They also shared their parents' multi-dimensional cultural norm preferences for food, turning away from pork and alcohol; they also had friends and acquaintances from Arabic and non-Arabic groups, and they enjoyed listening to music from different cultures as well.

**Summary**

In consequence of the interviews, it is apparent that the Arabic families are attempting to negotiate their roles in the United States Public School System; the need for multicultural education is important, mainly because the U. S. is a pluralistic society, one whose citizens possess a multitude of richly diverse cultures. The Arabic community is an important element of this pluralistic society, and from my interviews, it is apparent that they are searching for a voice in the United States Public School System. Consequently, the school systems need to include the Arabic voice in its curricula. Indeed, curriculum assimilation, the teachers lack of knowledge concerning the Arabic culture, stereotyping, cultural shock, and the expression of a need for multicultural education were discovered through my findings.

# CHAPTER 5

# IMPLICATIONS AND RECOMMENDATIONS

**Implications**

The single–continuum model of acculturation is described as the changing of an ethnic traditional cultural trait for Anglo cultural traits. The exchange of cultural traits results in an individual becoming more like the Anglo culture, and it is represented as a point on a continuum ranging from being unacculturated, bicultural, to acculturated (Ponterotto, 2001).

This qualitative study detailed the cultural and linguistic acculturation of Arabic families and their children in Pecan Valley, New Mexico, Green City, New York, Hot City, Texas, and Intermountain City, Utah, and it was aimed toward discovering what sorts of feelings that these processes had on them; chief among them was fear over losing their culture and language. Indeed, my findings (Table 5) found that most of the parents worried about the future of their children for a variety of reasons, a few of which were:

1. The fact that school curriculum focused on the students' assimilation into the dominant groups' language and culture.
2. The lack of knowledge that the teachers had concerning Arabic student backgrounds.
3. Stereotyping of Arabic people
4. The need for multicultural education.
5. Cultural Shock

In the public schools, the curriculum focused on the assimilation of different groups, including Arabic students; they were forced to use the English language as their primary form of communication all day long. English was encouraged while the students' first language was silenced. The students were forced into speaking English in English-only programs or English and Spanish in Bilingual programs. Consequently, language domination silenced the students' first language and forced them to speak the dominant group language, creating language assimilation in the process.

The culture of the Arabic students was also denied in public schools because the minority students, including the Arabic culture, assimilated into the dominant culture, consequently marginalizing the Arabic heritage. I agree with Stanley Aronowitz and Henry Giroux (1985) when they describe the function of the public schools' hidden curriculum as:

> The dominant school culture functions not only to legitimate interests and values of dominant groups; it also functions to marginalize and disconfirm knowledge forms and experiences that are extremely important to subordinate and oppressed groups. (p. 174)

In studying the Arabic students in public schools through classroom observations and teachers' interviews, I concluded that, in addition to the public school curriculum's lack of acknowledgement of the Arabic culture and language, the teachers also ignored the Arabic heritage, mainly because of their ignorance of the Arab world, whether it be geographical, cultural, etc.

Culture awareness and language loyalty were obvious among parents. Language and culture loyalty were rises up when the parent afraid of their children will lose their Arabic heritage of language and culture. They like to use English at the same time they want to read, write and speak Arabic. Parents and children prefer to interact with people from other ethnicities. In addition to daily life stress (environment, work/school, health and financial issues) families of Arab American face acculturative stress from immigration status, culture shock and minority status (Padilla, 1986, p.101-120).

Stereotyping was something else that the Arabic families and their children faced in and out of the school systems. Stereotyping, in my opinion, is epidemic, resulting from the media's portrayal of the Arabic people as ignorant, terrorists, women abusers, etc. Antonia Darder (1991) concludes that stereotyping of subordinate groups by dominant groups is used to justify social, political, and economic inequity, proclaiming that "Stereotyping of subordinate groups reflect the deep-rooted prejudices of the dominant culture that work to justify and sustain political, social, and economic inequity" (p. 41), later stating that "Racial stereotypes fuel misconceptions of subordinate cultures as inferior and imprison bicultural students and their communities into hardened images that influence the manner in which they are treated in schools and in society at large" (p. 41).

In the United States, the idea of multicultural education grew from the social movements of the 1960s and 1970s, mainly because this was a time when various groups protested and demanded for a change from the oppression that minority groups had often experienced. Indeed, there was a growing awareness that the discrimination against and exclusion of groups based on their race or gender was unacceptable, especially since it was clear that the United States was a pluralistic society, one that had much to offer if it included and acknowledged all of its people's contributions. Margaret Bustamante (1998) elaborates on multiculturalism by explaining,

> As a concept, multiculturalism recognizes cultural diversity as a fact of life in American society; knows the unique needs of students who are socially, culturally and linguistically different; understands that cultural groups are both similar and different, and rejects both the overemphasis of similarities within the groups and the differences among the groups. (p. 74)

Bustamente continues, explaining that "Multiculturalism stands for change, institution changes, curriculum changes, interaction changes, and mind changes" (p. 75), consequently revealing the necessity for multicultural education, mainly because all individuals deserve educational opportunities and chances to become productive individuals in society. Thus, the exclusion of the Arabic identity in the multicultural curriculum is something that must be addressed and corrected within the school and societal spheres.

Indeed, the inclusion of Arabic student voices within the United States School System is an essential key to their self-esteem and identities, especially since the number of Arabic students is growing fast; in order to broaden the scope of multicultural education, an observance of Muslim holidays and heroes would be helpful, thus improving the perception that Arabic individuals have within the social consciousness of the United States. This is an important step considering Islam is the second largest religion within this country, and Sonia Nieto (2000) explains that the students

> lack of understanding of cultures different from their own, the preconceptions they and their families may have brought from other countries, their internalizing of the negative ways in which differences are treated in our society, and the lack of information provided in the schools all serve to magnify the problem (p. 326)

that occurs when a culture is not represented in the classroom. She contends that "only by reforming the entire school environment can substantive changes in attitudes, behaviors, and achievements take place" (p. 326).

Multicultural education helps change any negative attitudes that students may hold against their Arabic classmates, and the parents interviewed in this study believe that multicultural education is a way in which they can preserve their language and culture, consequently ensuring that their children will not dissolve completely into the culture, values, morals, and ambitions of the dominant groups. As the school population continues to become more pluralistic, the demand for change increases, necessitating the need for multiculturalism. Another first-grade teacher expressed the need for multicultural education when she said,

"We need multicultural education in schools. We need families to communicate with us. We need diversity and the school to work with the community to have rich children."

In order to see multiculturalism happen, teaching candidates must experience effectively coordinated programs and coursework, consequently preparing themselves for their future lives in pluralistic classrooms. Indeed, the teachers' responses during our interviews have led me to believe that they too wish to enrich their knowledge by attending workshops and courses about multicultural education.

However, courses are not presently available to include all minority groups in the public school systems, a fact that one second-grade teacher is attempting to rectify, stating,

"I am planning to grow and take some classes at the university to enrich my knowledge with children from all cultures' training and schooling."

The institutions should ensure that their prospective teachers are qualified in academic, linguistic, and cultural issues, thus creating an environment where multicultural education can flourish. One high-school teacher verbalized the importance of multicultural education by voicing:

> The need for instruction should start from the very top, beginning with how my boss treats the people in poverty, disabled, or other different groups; people tend to follow that whether they agree or not. All adults in the school culture are looking at every kid individually, and students are looking at the people in charge; you will be surprised by how the student models after the people who run the country.
> Another high-school teacher said,

". . . we need the people in power, people who hire teachers, to start looking at hiring the right people to positions who believe that all people are individuals, to present people who want to learn about others and look outside of the self and be open-minded."

Another teacher expressed her desire for cultural sensitivity courses with:

> I think I need to attend multicultural sensitivity training programs to learn more about other cultures so I can avoid hurting students without knowing it. Also, I think it is very important for us as educators to become more aware of

the other cultures. We need the help and participation of the Arabic community. We really need to encourage help from parents.

In sum, multicultural education is for all students, and it should help them understand their languages, cultures, and communities' cultures. Presently, Arabic students are excluded from multicultural education, consequently necessitating the need to reevaluate the school systems; through this reexamination, education will hopefully incorporate multiculturalism within all school system programs, something that Hakuta and Bialystok (1994) desire, remarking, "We cannot hope to understand ourselves and our own place in this world without understanding the enormous impact of linguistic and cultural diversity on the human social condition" (p. 10).

Cultural shock is "the process of initial adjustment to an unfamiliar environment . . . [it] has been used to describe the adjustment process in its emotional, psychological, behavioral, cognitive, and physiological impact on individuals" (Pedersen, 1995, p. 1). It is one of the main problems that the Arabic students face when they come from the schools in the Middle East countries; their patterns of social life are different, especially in gender relations, clothing, the head scarf, food, and violence. Very rarely does violence happen in Middle Eastern school campuses.

**Recommendations**

The American public schools are growing with increasing numbers of multi-ethnic individuals. The student populations represent different cultural backgrounds, and many students now speak languages other than English in consequence. Since Arabic students factor in as one of the major populations in public schools, they and their parents have expressed the need for a curriculum that honors their cultural backgrounds. In reference to the conclusions of the study, many recommendations are suggested to improve the Arabic children's learning processes in the public schools.

For one, the public schools should be reconstructed to honor diverse student populations, including Arabic students. Darder (1991) expressed:

> Critical educators of bicultural students must consider creative ways in which they can work to restructure public school environments that support experiences of culturally democratic life. The manner in which this is done must take into account not only the specific needs that bicultural students bring into the classroom, but also the needs that teachers have in order to be more effective educators. (p. 123)

A multicultural curriculum is needed in public school classrooms, and it must relate to the students, parents, communities, and schools. The need for a multicultural program that promotes the students' active voice, dialogue, and participation within the schools is imperative. Also, multicultural curriculum should include better systems of evaluating the multicultural students, replacing its traditional methods in consequence. Sonia Nieto (2000) explains that

> students' lack of understanding of cultures different from their own, the preconceptions they and their families have brought from other countries, their internalizing of the negative ways in which differences are treated in our society, and the lack of information provided in the schools all serve to magnify the problem. (p. 326)

Indeed, many of the parents and students that I interviewed expressed the desire for multicultural classrooms that would embrace their Arabic heritage.

School funding is also essential for multicultural programs in the public schools. Indeed, Grant and Tate (1995) explain that "a key factor in the development of long-term and sustained multicultural education research is funding" (p. 158). Money is needed to support schools, providing resources to help the students, parents, and teachers achieve decent educations through funding provided for multicultural education programs. Some of the interviewed teachers in the public schools touched on the school's lack of funding, indicating that more would be needed in order to encourage multiculturalism. Also, I have to mention that private funding is needed from Arab communities to raise money for schooling their children in Arabic schools and multi-educational programs. So, Proposals for getting funds is something important to get help from the Arab countries to help the schools around the country.

Also, the colleges have an important role in preparing future teachers. More multicultural courses are thus needed in universities to address all of the cultures in the public schools; it is important to academically prepare future teachers for diverse school populations, teaching them cultural sensitivity in the process. Ellwood (1995) declares,

> Too many teacher education programs fail to train teachers to address the deep complexities of human interaction that teaching really involves. When cultural differences compound these complexities, the need for sophisticated teacher training is even greater. (p. 251)

The teacher's role at the public schools is to be a guide to their students. The teacher must enable their students to view and understand other cultures existing in the world. In adapting the critical theory approaches (Ellwood, 1995), the teachers should be like transformative intellectuals, individuals capable of transforming the world critically, thus teaching their students to be transformer agents for their lives. It is recommended that teachers get the necessary training and skills to work with multicultural students like the Arabic students.

The gap separating public schools, parents, and communities should be reduced. As a result of this study, I have found that there was a lack of communication between schools and the Arabic families. The participation of the parents was very limited; the public schools should have encouraged the parents to participate more in the schooling of their children. The parents' participation in school projects may help decrease the stereotypical image of the Arab world in and out of the schools' social environments. The involvement of parents within the schools and the communities may empower the teachers', students', and parents' learning processes. Trumbull, et al. (2001) declares that there is a "mountain of research showing that parent involvement contributes significantly to student achievement and other positive outcomes" (p. 29). Also, it is recommended that the school personnel, teachers, and parents set up objectives and goals for the multicultural programs, ones that include Arabic students as well as others.

As the public school populations continue to grow, the need for more research comes to the surface. Through research, the people in charge can effectively improve education, something that Berliner and Biddle (1997) champion in their book, The

Manufactured Crises, emphasizing the need for more research in the American public school systems. They state:

> As Americans turns away from these damaging ideas, we will want to address the real issues that the public schools of our country face-issues that are tied to serious and growing social problems in the nation. And as we debate ways to address these issues and plan programs that we hope will improve our schools, we should remember that reforms in education are far more effective when they are based on knowledge derived from research. Research is not frill; rather, it is badly needed if our efforts to improve public schools are to be effective. (p. 350)

For future research, it will be useful to conduct follow up studies on the acculturation of Arab American students in the United States and to address the issues of stereotyping, cultural shock, gender, racism, prejudice, discrimination, social class, acculturation with different ethnic minorities. Findings from the current study suggest strong relations between the acculturation process and the above issues, which are facing the Arab students under the public school system. There have been no systematic studies on Arab American population in connection with stereotyping, cultural shock, gender, racism, social class, and acculturation with different ethnic minorities. Therefore, further research is needed to address each of these issues in deep details. Also, it worth to mention that it is always beneficial to tie these future studies to Multicultural education as a mean to understand all ethnic minorities in the United States within acculturation process.

Stereotyping is one of the finding that Arab American considers it as an epidemic. In my study it was one of the repeated findings through the study of acculturation of Arabic families and their children in the United States. It was repeated in the findings of the parents' interviews, the children and focus group interviews. Little been done through research to deal in depth with issues of stereotyping. This will be one of my recommendations for future research to study stereotyping as a phenomena and its deep-rooted effect in the process of acculturation of the parents and their children in the United States.

Cultural shock was one of the findings that generate from the difference between American dominant culture and Arab world culture. For future recommendations based on my study, more in-depth research is needed to address this issue with first and second generations of Arab American. Cultural shock still a phenomena that not yet been investigated within acculturation of Arabic communities in America. Lack of information will keep cultural gap between Arab American and other surroundings communities.

Gender and social class are of the important dimensions of our American society. Gender issues within acculturation of Arab American are still missing from literature and consequently from research. Gender within Arab families has different rules for male sand females. It is important to understand the acculturation process for both Arabic genders. Also, it is important to understand how gender differences been influenced differently within acculturation of Arab American in stereotyping and cultural shock and social class.

For Future considerations of acknowledging Arabic people, more studies will be needed to relate issues of racism, prejudice and discrimination to acculturation of Arabic American within American society. These three issues are still affecting the

Arab American communities, but nothing is done to research such dimensions in relation to acculturation process of Arabic people.

Finally, it is worth mentioning for more studies to be conduct in acculturation of Arabic people and other American ethnicities. This qualitative study addresses mainly one model of acculturation the single-continuum model. My study interviews of parents and children in preference to language and culture show interest of Arab American interactions with other ethnic minorities. More studies needed in that area of acculturation and other different minorities of the United States.

**Limitations of the Study**

I have experienced many difficulties and limitations when I was conducting the study. Among these are the following factors:

1. Fear Factor: After Sep11, the mode of many of my sample populations was changed, and it became difficult to gather data regarding politics, racism and discrimination. People expressed fears when they spoke about their experiences with the education process in the school system.
2. Limitation of states included in my study. Although the four states included in my study were chosen from different parts of the country, it was still limited to small number of families in comparison to the total number of Arabs who lived in the United Sates. My study was only conducted in New Mexico, Texas, Utah and New York, where there is large enough Arab population for a study sample. However, further

studies are recommended in other states to provide for a better understating of the acculturation process for the majority of Arab communities in the United States.

3. The sample population was limited to families and students within the family. However, samples from outside family boundaries, like independent students who lived on their own, could acculturate differently.

4. Religious limitations: All my targeted populations were Arab-Muslims. However, there were not Arab-Christians or other Arab faith families available in the areas of my study. Therefore, more study may be needed to cover the acculturation of non-Muslim Arab families.

5. Geographic and demographic factors: Participants are limited to certain Arabic countries, and not all Arabic countries are represented as a result.

**APPENDICES**

# APPENDIX A

## ARAB WORLD MAP

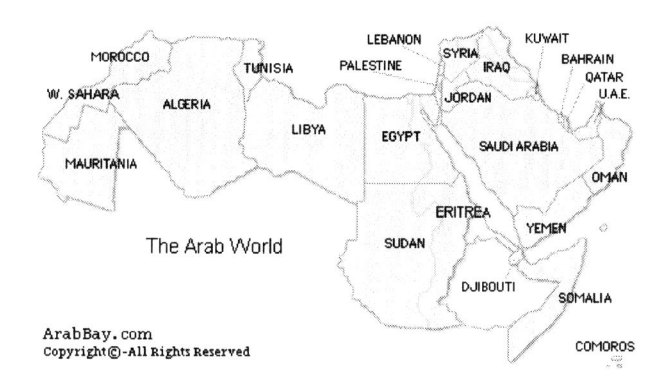

http://www.arabbay.com/arabmap.htm

## APPENDIX B

### INTERVIEWING USING SEIDMAN PROCEDURE WITH
### 4 TUTORS, 14 TEACHERS, 3 PRINCIPALS

1. (History of acculturation) What history do you have with Arabic children?

2. (Experience of acculturation) What are your actual duties regarding multicultural education?

3. (Future of acculturation) What is your understanding of being a bi-lingual teacher? What sense does it make?

## APPENDIX C

## OPEN-ENDED INTERVIEW QUESTIONS WITH STUDENTS
## OF MIDDLE AND HIGH SCHOOLS

1. How you feel about your school?
2. What do you think of your school?
3. What do you like best about your school?
4. How do you feel about your teachers?
5. What was your first impression of the school's curriculum?
6. What do you like best about the curriculum?
7. Are there any parts of the curriculum you do not like?
8. Does your teacher encourage you to participate in class?
9. If you were in charge, what would you want to change in curriculum?
10. Does the curriculum encourage you to talk about your culture, language, and values?
11. What advice or changes would you make to the curriculum?
12. What else do you want to tell me about the school's curriculum?

## APPENDIX D

### FOCUS GROUP QUESTIONS FOR (FATHERS GROUP) OF 15 PARENTS OF PRE-SCHOOL, ELEMENTARY, MIDDLE AND HIGH SCHOOLS STUDENTS

1. What do you think of the school's curriculum?

2. How do you feel about the parents' conferences?

3. What do you like best about the school?

4. How do you feel about your children's teachers?

5. Are there any problems in school?

6. What barriers exist?

7. Does the school give any attention to your children's culture and /or language?

8. What should the school be concerned with?

9. How should the decision be made regarding your child's education?

10. Is there any advice you have for the school's administrators?

11. What can each of us do?

12. What can we do as a group?

**APPENDIX E**

OPEN-ENDED INTERVIEW QUESTIONS OF LANGUAGE PREFERENCE
WITH STUDENTS AND THEIR PARENTS

1. Do you prefer to speak Arabic or English?

2. Do you prefer to read Arabic or in English?

3. Do you prefer to write Arabic or English?

4. Do you prefer reading Arabic or English newspapers and magazines?

5. Do you prefer listening to Arabic or to English radio stations?

6. Do you prefer watching Arabic or English television stations?

7. Do you prefer going to Arabic or to English movies?

8. What language do you prefer to speak at your social gatherings?

9. What language do you prefer to use with most of your friends?

10. What language do you prefer to use when you are talking about a personal or emotional problem with a relative?

11. What language do you prefer to use when you are angry?

12. Do you prefer to carry on conversations every day in English or Arabic?

13. What language do you prefer to speak at home?

14. What language you prefer to learn to speak at school?

15. Do you prefer to buy or subscribe to Arabic or to English newspapers and magazines?

## APPENDIX F

### OPEN-ENDED INTERVIEW QUESTIONS OF CULTURAL PREFERENCE WITH STUDENTS AND THEIR PARENT

1. Do you prefer to think of yourself as American?

2. Do you prefer to think yourself as Arab American?

3. Do you prefer to think yourself as Arabic?

4. Do you prefer to attend the Islamic Centers?

5. Do you prefer to eat Arabic food?

6. Do you prefer to eat American food?

7. Do you prefer to eat Arabic food on holidays?

8. Do you prefer to eat at Arabic restaurant?

9. Do you prefer to marry from Arabic descent?

10. Do you prefer that Arabic women to wear a headscarf?

11. Do you prefer that children of Arabic descent should learn about Arabic history in American schools?

12. Do you think that there is a better chance of getting ahead in the U.S. than in country of origin?

13. Do you think that a child growing up in the U.S. is luckier than a child growing up in country of origin?

14. Do you think that the most delicious food is American food?

15. Do you think that the best music is the Arabic music?

16. If you could take a trip, would you rather travel to your country of origin?

17. Are your friends mostly of Arabic descent?
18. Are your friends of mixed ethnicities?
19. Are your neighbors mostly of Arabs?
20. Are your neighbors mostly of Anglo descent?
21. Are your neighbors of mixed ethnicities?
22. Are the people at the places where you go to (parties, picnics) mostly of Arabic descent?
23. Are the people at the places where you go to (parties, picnics) mostly of Anglo descent?
24. Are the people at the places where you go to (parties, picnics) mostly of mixed descent?

# REFERENCES

Al-Khatab, A. (1999). In Search of Equity for Arab-Americans Students in Public Schools of the United States. *Education, 120*, 254-66.

All About the Arabic Language. (2002). The American Association of Teachers of Arabic. Retrieved April 25, 2002, from http://www.wm.edu/nata

Appelbaum, P. (2002). *Multicultural and Diversity Education*. Santa Barbara: ABC-CLIO.

ArabBay.com (2001). The Arab World. Retrieved April 25, 2002, from http://www.arabbay.com/arabmap.htm

Aronowitz, S., & Giroux, H. (1985). *Education Under Siege*. New York: Bergin & Garvey.

Banks, J. A. (1981). *Multiethnic Education and Theory*. Boston: Allyn and Bacon.

Banks, J. A. (1988). *Multiethnic Education: Theory and Practice* (2nd ed.). Boston: Allyn & Bacon.

Banks, J. A. (1996). The African American Roots of Multicultural Education. In J. A. Banks (Ed.), *Multicultural Education: Transformative Knowledge and Action*. (pp 30-45). New York: Teachers College Press.

Bhola, H.S. (1990). *Evaluation "Literacy for Development" Projects, Programs and Campaigns: Evaluating, Planning, Design and Implementation and Utilization of Evaluation Results*. Hamburg, Germany: Unesco Institute for Education.

Berk, R. (Ed.) (1981). *Educational Evaluation Methodology: The State of The Art*. Baltimore: Johns Hopkins University Press.

Berry, J. W. (1980). Acculturation as Varieties of Adoption. In A. M. Padilla (Ed.), *Acculturation: Theory, Models, and Some New Findings* (pp. 9-25). Boulder: Westview Press.

Berliner, D. C., & Biddle, B. J. (1997). *The Manufactured Crisis: Myths, Fraud, and the Attack on America's Public Schools*. White Plains, NY: Longman.

Bogdan, R. & Biklen, S (1998). *Qualitative Research for Education: An Introduction to Theory and Methods* (3rd ed). Boston: Allyn and Bacon.

Bucher, R. D. (1999). *Diversity Consciousness*. Englewood Cliffs, NJ: Prentice Hall.

Bustamante, M. (1998). Multicultural Education. In S. Marx (Ed.), Challenging the Culture of Education (pp. 74-77). EDUC 604, New Mexico State University, Las Cruces, NM: Special Report.

Dana, R. H. (2000). An Assessment-Intervention Model for Research and Practice with Multicultural Population. In I. B. Wiener (Ed.), *Personality and Clinical Psychology Series*. Mahwah, NJ: Lawrence Erlbaum Associates.

Darder, A. (1991). *Culture and Power in the Classroom: A Critical Foundation for Bicultural Education*. New York: Bergin & Garvey.

De George, G. (Ed.) (1985). *Bilingual Program Management: A Problem Solving Approach*. Cambridge: Evaluation and Assessment Center for Bilingual Education.

Denzin, N. K., & Lincoln, Y. S. (Eds.) (1994). *Handbook of Qualitative Research.* Thousand Oaks, CA: Sage Publications.

Denzin, N. K., & Lincoln, Y. S. (Eds.) (1998). *Collecting and Interpreting Qualitative Materials.* Thousand Oaks, CA: Sage Publications.

Dohrenwend, B. P., & Smith, R. J. (1962). Toward a Theory of Acculturation. *Southwestern Journal of Anthropology,* 18, 30-39.

Ellwood, C. (1995). Preparing Teachers for Education in a Diverse World. In D. Levine, et al. (Eds.). *Rethinking Schools.* New York: The New Press.

Feagin, J. R., & Booher, C. (2003). *Racial and Ethnic Relations* (7th ed.). Upper Saddle River, NJ: Prentice Hall.

Fisher, W. B. (1987). *The Middle East and North Africa.* London: Europa Publications.

Freire, P. (1993). *Pedagogy of the Oppressed.* New York: Continuum Press.

Gordon, M. M. (1964). *Assimilation in American Life.* London: Oxford University Presss.

Grant, C. A., & Tate, W. F. (1995). Multicultural Education Through the Lens of the Multicultural Education Research Literature. In J. A. Banks (Ed.), *Handbook of Research on Multicultural Education* (p. 158). New York: Simon & Shuster Macmillan.

Gredler, M. E. (1996). *Program Evaluation.* Englewood Clifffs, NJ: Merrill.

Griswold, J. W. (1975). *The Image of the Middle East In Secondary School Textbooks.* New York: Middle East Studies Association of North America.

Guba, E. G., & Lincoln, Y. S. (1989). *Fourth Generation Evaluation.* Newbury Park, CA: Sage Publications.

Haneef, S. (2000). *What Every One Should Know About Islam and Muslim.* New Delhi, India: Noida Printing Press.

Harris, P. R., & Moran, R. T. (1996). *Managing Cultural Differences* (4th ed.). Houston: Gulf Publishing.

Hakuta & Bialystok (1994). *In Other Worlds.* New York: Basic Books.

Herskovits, J. M. (1938). *Acculturation: The Study of Culture Contact.* New York: J. J Augustin.

Hill, J. C. (1986). *Curriculum Evaluation for School Improvement.* Springfield, IL: Charles C Thomas Publisher.

House, E. R. (1993). *Professional Evaluation: Social Impact and Political Consequences.* Newbury, CA: Sage Publications.

Islam.com (2000). Retrieved April 20, 2002, from http://www.islam.com

Jarrar, S. A. (1983). The Treatment of Arabs in U.S. Social Studies Textbooks. In E. Ghareeb (Ed.), *Split Vision: The Portrayal of Arabs in the American Media* (pp. 381-390). Washington, DC: American Arab-Affairs Councils.

The Joint Committee on Standards for Educational Evaluation (1981). *Standards for Evaluations of Educational Programs, Projects and Materials.* New York: McGraw-Hill.

The Joint Committee on Standards for Educational Evaluation (1994). *The Program Evaluation Standards* (2nd ed.). Thousand Oaks, CA: Sage Publications.

Jorgensen, D. L. (1989). *Participant Observer: A Methodology for Human Resources.* Newbury Park, CA: Sage Publications

Krueger, R. (1994). *Focus Groups: A Practical Guide for Applied Research* (2nd ed.). Thousand Oaks, CA: Sage Publications.

Krueger, R. (1998). *Focus Groups Kit.* Thousands Oaks, CA: Sage Publications.

Kuhn, T. S. (1970). *The Structure of Scientific Revolutions* (2nd ed.). Chicago: University of Chicago Press.

Lambert, W. E., & Taylor, D. M. (1990). *Coping with Cultural and Racial Diversity in Urban America.* New York: Praeger.

Lloyd, W and Srole, L. (1945). *The Social System of American Ethnic Groups.* New Haven: Yale University Press.

Madaus, G. F., Scriven, M., & Stufflebeam, D. L. (1983). Program Evaluation: A Historical Overview. In G. F. Madaus, M. Scriven, & D. L. Stufflebeam (Eds.), *Evaluation Models: Viewpoints on Educational and Human Service Evaluation* (pp. 3-22) Boston: Kluwer-Nijhoff Publishing.

Marshall, C., & Rossman, G. (1989). *Designing Qualitative Research.* Newbury Park, CA: Sage Publications.

Mohl, R. (1991). Cultural Assimilation Versus Cultural Pluralism. In G. E. Pozzetta (Ed.), *Assimilation, Acculturation and Social Mobility* (Vol. 13, p. 188). New York: Garland Publishing.

Morgan, D. (1998). *The Focus Group Kit: The Focus Group Guidebook.* Thousand Oaks, CA: Sage Publications.

Moore, J. W., & Pachon, H. (1985). *Hispanics in the United States.* Englewood Cliffs, NJ: Prentice Hall.

Nassar-McMillan, S. C., & J. Hakim-Larson (2003). Counseling Considerations Among Arab Americans. *Journal of Counseling & Development, 81,* 150-159.

Nieto, S. (2000). *Affirming Diversity* (3rd ed.). New York: Addison Wesley Longman.

Nieto, S. (2002). *Language, Culture, and Teaching.* Mahwah, NJ: Lawrence Erlbaum Associates.

Olmedo, E. L. (1979). Acculturation: A Psychometric Perspective. *American Psychologist, 34,* 1061-1070.

100 Questions and Answers about Arab Americans: A Journalist's Guide (2001). Detroit Free Press. Retrieved April 24, 2002, from http//www.freep.com/jobspage/arabs/index.htm

Padilla, M. A. (1986). *Acculturation and Stress Among Immigrants and Later Generation Individuals* In the Quality of Urban Life. (pp. 101-120). New York, NY: Walter de Gruyter & Co. New York.

Patai, R. (1969). *On Culture Contact And Its Working In Modern Palestine.* New York: Kraus Reprint.

Patai, R. (2002). *The Arab Mind.* New York: Hatherleigh Press.

Patton, M. Q. (1990). *Qualitative Evaluation and Research Methods* (2nd ed.). Newbury Park, CA: Sage Publications.

Pedersen, P. (1995). *The Five Stages of Culture Shock*. Westport, CT: Greenwood Press.

Ponterotto, J. G., Casas, J. M., Suzuki, L. A. & Alexander, C. M. (2001). *Handbook of Multicultural Counseling* (2nd ed.) (pp. 394-421). Thousands Oaks, CA: Sage Publications.

Portilla, L. M. (1990). *Endangered Cultures*. Dallas: Southern Methodist Press.

Rallis, S. F., & Rossman, G. B. (1998). *Learning in the Field: An Introduction to Qualitative Research*. Thousands Oaks, CA: Sage Publications.

Roysircar-Sodowsky, G. & Maestas, M. V. (2000). Acculturation, Ethnic Identity, and Acculturative Stress: Evidence and Measurement. In I. B. Weiner (Ed.), *Personality and Clinical Psychology Series* (p.135). Mahwah, NJ: Lawrence Erlbaum Associates.

Seidman, I. (1998). *Interviewing as Qualitative Research: A Guide for Researchers in Education and The Social Sciences* (2nd ed.). New York: Teachers College Press.

Shaheen, J. G. (1999). Hollywood's Muslim Arabs [Electronic version]. *The Muslim World*, 90 (1/2), 22-42.

The Social Science Research Council Summer Seminar on Acculturation (1954). Acculturation: An Exploratory Formulation. *American Anthropologist, 56*, 973-1002.

Spindler, L.S. (1977). *Culture Change and Modernization: Mini-models and Case Studies*. New York: Holt, Rinehart and Winston.

Stirk, P. M. (2000). *Critical Theory, Politics and Society*. London: Pinter.

Stufflebeam, D. (1983). The CIPP Model for Program Evaluation. In G. F. Madaus, M. Scriven, & D. Stufflebeam (Eds.), *Evaluation Models: Viewpoints on Educational and Human Service Evaluation* (pp. 117-141). Boston: Kluwer-Nijhoff.

Stufflebeam, D., Foley, W., Gephart, W., Guba, E., Hammond, R., Merriman., & Provus, M. (1971). *Educational Evaluation & Decision Making*. Itasca, IL: F. E. Peacock Publishers.

Szapocznik, J., & Kurtines, W. (1980). Acculturation, Biculturalism and Adjustment among Cuban Americans. In A. M. Padilla (Ed), *Acculturation: Theory, Models and Some New Findings* (p. 139-159). Boulder: Westview Press.

Trumbull, E., et al. (2001). *Bridging Cultures*. Mahwah, NJ: Lawrence Erlbaum Associates.

Uwe, F. (1998). *An Introduction to Qualitative Research*. Thousand Oaks, CA: Sage Publications.

Warner, L., & Srole, L. (1945). *The Social System of American Ethnic Groups*. New Haven: Yale University Press.

Worthen, B. R., & Sanders, J. R. (1987). *Educational Evaluation: Alternative Approaches and Practical Guidelines*. New York: Longman.

Zintz, V. M. (1969). *Education Across Culture* (2nd ed.). Dubuque, IA:Kendall/Hunt.

**VDM** publishing **house ltd.**

# Scientific Publishing House

offers

# free of charge publication

of current academic research papers, Bachelor´s Theses, Master's Theses, Dissertations or Scientific Monographs

If you have written a thesis which satisfies high content as well as formal demands, and you are interested in a remunerated publication of your work, please send an e-mail with some initial information about yourself and your work to *info@vdm-publishing-house.com*.

Our editorial office will get in touch with you shortly.

**VDM Publishing House Ltd.**
Meldrum Court 17.
Beau Bassin
Mauritius
www.vdm-publishing-house.com